Bratislava Travel Guide 2025

Ružinov: Parks, Lakes, and Local Life, The Old Town, Devin Castle and the Danube River Views, Hiking in the Small Carpathians, Day Trip to Vienna.

By

Rachel J. Pugh

Copyright © 2025 by Rachel J. Pugh, All rights reserved.

No part of this publication may be reproduced, distributed, or transmitted in any form or by any means, including photocopying, recording, or other electronic or mechanical methods, without the prior written permission of the publisher, except in the case of brief quotations embodied in critical reviews and certain other noncommercial uses permitted by copyright law.

Disclaimer: The information provided in this book is for general informational purposes only. While the author has endeavored to ensure the accuracy of the content, he assumes no responsibility for errors or omissions, or for any damages resulting from the use of the information contained herein.

Trademark Disclaimer: All product names, logos, and brands mentioned in this book are property of their respective owners. All company, product, and service names used in this book are for identification purposes only. Use of these names, logos, and brands does not imply endorsement.

Table of Contents

Chapter 1. Introduction ... 8
   Welcome to Bratislava ... 8
   Overview of Bratislava ... 10
   A Brief History of the City ... 11
   Why Visit Bratislava? ... 13
   Best Time to Visit ... 16

Chapter 2. Planning Your Trip ... 18
   Visa and Travel Requirements ... 18
   Currency and Customs ... 20
   Customs and Etiquette in Bratislava ... 21

Chapter 3. Getting There ... 23
   By Air: Bratislava Airport ... 23
   By Train: Rail Connections to Major Cities ... 25
   By Bus and Car: Transportation Options ... 27

Chapter 4. Getting Around ... 31
   Trams ... 31
   Buses ... 33
   Taxis ... 36
   Bicycles ... 39

Chapter 5. Top Attractions ... 42
   Bratislava Castle ... 42
   St. Martin's Cathedral ... 44
   The Blue Church (Church of St. Elizabeth) ... 47
   Slovak National Gallery and Museum ... 50
   The UFO Observation Deck ... 53
   Primate's Palace ... 56
   Devin Castle and the Danube River Views ... 58

Chapter 6. Exploring Bratislava's Neighborhoods ... 62
   The Old Town: Charm and History ... 62
   Petržalka: Modern City Vibes ... 64
   Nové Mesto: Bratislava's Growing District ... 65
   Ružinov: Parks, Lakes, and Local Life ... 67

Chapter 7. Culture and Entertainment ... 72
   Slovak Traditions and Folklore ... 72
   Festivals and Events: What's Happening in Bratislava ... 74
   Folk Art Festival (Východné Folklore Festival) ... 76
   Bratislava International Film Festival ... 79
   Pohoda Festival ... 81
   The Arts: Galleries and Theaters, and Music Venues ... 84
   Theaters: ... 89
   Music Venues: ... 94

Chapter 8. Where to Eat and Drink	99
Traditional Slovak Cuisine: Must-Try Dishes	99
Best Restaurants for Every Budget	102
Slovak Drinks: Wine, Beer, and Liquor	**107**
Chapter 9. Shopping and Souvenirs	109
Best Shopping Streets and Malls	109
Markets: Where to Find Authentic Souvenirs	112
Chapter 10. Outdoor Adventures	117
Hiking in the Small Carpathians	117
Chapter 11. Day Trips from Bratislava	120
The Small Carpathian Wine Region	120
Day Trip to Vienna (Austria)	121
The Town of Trnava	123
The Hungarian Border: A Quick Trip to Komárno	125
Chapter 12. Practical Travel Tips	128
Safety and Health Information	128
Chapter 13. Suggested Itineraries	131
2-Day Itinerary: Exploring the Heart of the City	131
4-Day Itinerary: A Deeper Dive into Bratislava	133
Family-Friendly Itinerary: Activities for All Ages	137
Romantic Weekend Getaway	141
Chapter 14. Resources	144
Useful Websites and Apps	144
Contact Information for Tourist Offices and Services	147
Bonus	150
Travel Journal	**152**

Chapter 1. Introduction

Welcome to Bratislava

Welcome to Bratislava! A city full of charm and history, a place where the past meets the present, and where every corner tells its own unique story. I remember the first time I arrived here, and it felt like stepping into a hidden gem, often overlooked but brimming with character. I instantly felt that this city, with its cobblestone streets, impressive castles, and welcoming people, had a way of drawing you in and making you feel right at home.

As I walked through the streets of the Old Town, I couldn't help but notice the mix of architectural styles. The medieval buildings, with their colorful facades and narrow lanes, seemed to whisper tales of times gone by. The atmosphere was lively yet calm, with cafés spilling out onto the streets and the sound of music drifting from the nearby squares.

One of my first stops was the iconic Bratislava Castle, perched high above the city with sweeping views of the Danube River. Standing there, looking out over the city and beyond to neighboring Austria, I felt a deep sense of history. The castle has seen centuries of change, and yet it still stands proudly as a symbol of Bratislava's strength and resilience. It's hard not to feel inspired as you walk through its grounds, taking in the views and imagining what life must have been like for the kings and queens who once roamed these halls.

Another spot that quickly became one of my favorites is the Old Town. The winding streets are full of charm, with little surprises around every corner. From quaint little shops selling handmade crafts to the beautiful St. Martin's Cathedral, a place of quiet reflection, there's always something to discover. I spent hours wandering around, not needing a specific destination, just soaking in the atmosphere of this beautiful city. It was here that I truly understood the saying, "It's not about the destination, but the journey."

Then there's the UFO Observation Deck, which offers one of the best panoramic views of Bratislava. As I ascended the elevator to the top, I was excited to see the city from above. The modern design of the deck, with its futuristic shape, felt like a sharp contrast to the historic architecture below. But in a way, it brought everything together. You could see how Bratislava balances the old and new, blending history with modernity in a way that feels completely natural.

And of course, no visit to Bratislava is complete without a stroll along the Danube River. Whether you're sitting by the water, watching the boats go by, or taking a river cruise, the Danube is an essential part of the city's identity. I took some time to sit by the riverbank, watching the sunset and thinking about how this river has connected people for centuries. It's moments like these that make you appreciate the quiet beauty of this city.

I want to take a moment to personally thank you for choosing to buy this book. There are so many travel guides out there, but you've trusted me to help you discover the best of Bratislava. That means a lot, and I'm honored to be part of your journey. Whether you're planning your first visit or coming back for more, I hope this guide provides you with the inspiration and knowledge you need to truly experience everything Bratislava has to offer. I'm excited for you to make your own memories here, to discover the hidden gems, to enjoy the food, the culture, and the warmth of the people. This city is special in so many ways, and I'm thrilled to share it with you.

Bratislava is a city that stays with you. It's not flashy or overrun by tourists, but that's part of its charm. It's a place where you can truly feel the pulse of history while enjoying the modern comforts of today. I'm sure you'll find that, like me, you'll fall in love with this wonderful city and all it has to offer.

Thank you again for choosing this book. Your journey through Bratislava is just beginning, and I can't wait for you to experience it all.

Overview of Bratislava

Overview of Bratislava

Bratislava, the capital of Slovakia, may not be as widely known as some of Europe's more famous capitals, but it holds a quiet charm that makes it unforgettable once you experience it. Nestled on the banks of the Danube River, this city is a unique blend of ancient history and modern flair, where medieval streets sit side by side with cutting-edge architecture. It's a place where the past is alive in the buildings, the cobblestone streets, and the stories of its people, yet the energy of the present is palpable, from its bustling cafés to its vibrant cultural scene.

Bratislava is compact, which is one of the things that makes it so special. In just a few days, you can experience the city in its entirety. The Old Town, with its narrow alleyways and beautiful squares, is a perfect starting point. It's here that you'll find some of the most iconic landmarks of the city, like Bratislava Castle, which towers over the city, offering spectacular views of the Danube River and beyond. From the Castle, you can easily see how the city is positioned at the crossroads of Central Europe — close to Austria and Hungary, with influences from all directions.

Though small, Bratislava is rich in history, and every building, monument, and street seems to have a story to tell. The city has witnessed the rise and fall of empires, including the Austro-Hungarian Empire, and it's reflected in the architecture. The Old Town is a perfect example of this, with its Baroque, Gothic, and Renaissance buildings standing in harmony. The Primate's Palace, with its beautiful hall, and St. Martin's Cathedral, one of the oldest buildings in the city, remind you of Bratislava's royal past, while the city's more modern architecture, like the UFO Observation Deck on the New Bridge, shows its contemporary spirit.

One of the striking things about Bratislava is how the city effortlessly balances old-world charm with modern convenience. Its small size means you're never far from any major attraction, and everything is walkable, which gives the city a cozy, intimate feel. Even the modern developments that have sprouted up in recent years, such as new shopping centers and stylish restaurants, blend seamlessly with the city's historic areas. It's a place where old and new meet in an exciting way.

Bratislava is also a city of culture. With its lively arts scene, rich traditions, and thriving music culture, it's impossible not to feel the creativity that pulses through the city. Whether it's attending a performance at the Slovak National Theatre, exploring the galleries that showcase Slovak art, or listening to local musicians perform in one of the many cafés, there's always something to see, hear, and do. The city is home to many festivals, too, from classical music festivals to quirky events like the Bratislava Food Festival, where visitors can taste Slovak cuisine and local specialties.

Despite being a capital, Bratislava feels manageable, comfortable, and not too overwhelming. There's a certain tranquility to it, a slower pace of life that invites you to linger a little longer, to wander the streets without rushing, and to take in the beauty around you. The people are warm and welcoming, always ready to share the history of their city, offer tips on where to eat, or simply chat over a cup of coffee.

And let's not forget the surrounding natural beauty. The city sits at the foot of the Little Carpathians mountain range, offering great opportunities for hiking and cycling. The Danube River, which flows through the heart of Bratislava, adds to the city's charm, with picturesque riverbanks, boat tours, and scenic paths that invite you to explore. The proximity of the countryside makes Bratislava the perfect base for day trips, whether it's visiting nearby castles or heading into neighboring Austria or Hungary for a quick getaway.

In many ways, Bratislava feels like a hidden treasure. It doesn't boast the crowds of tourists that flood other European capitals, but it offers just as much to see and experience. From its historic streets to its modern attractions, the warmth of its people to its breathtaking landscapes, Bratislava is a city that will capture your heart in the most unexpected ways.

If you haven't yet visited, I can't recommend it enough. And if you're already planning your trip, get ready to fall in love with this city that's as full of history as it is of life. Bratislava is waiting for you.

A Brief History of the City

History of Bratislava

Bratislava, Slovakia's capital, has a fascinating history that stretches back over a thousand years. The city's location at the crossroads of Central Europe, along the banks of the Danube River, has made it a significant cultural, political, and economic hub for centuries. Over the course of its long history, Bratislava has witnessed the rise and fall of empires, the ebb and flow of various civilizations, and the creation of a distinctive Slovak identity. Let's take a closer look at the history that has shaped this remarkable city.

Prehistoric and Ancient Periods

Bratislava's history dates back to prehistoric times, with evidence of human settlement in the area as early as the Bronze Age. Archaeological finds show that early settlers were drawn to the fertile land and the strategic position along the Danube River. The area was likely home to various Celtic tribes, who established settlements around the 4th century BC. One of the most significant prehistoric sites in the region is the Zlaté Moravce, an area that was inhabited by the Celts.

Following the Celtic period, the Romans arrived in the 1st century AD, establishing a military outpost along the Danube River known as Gerulata near the modern-day suburb of Rusovce. The Romans constructed forts and roads in the area, marking the region as an important military and trade route within the Roman Empire. While the Romans never fully settled the area that would become Bratislava, their presence undoubtedly left an impact on the city's early development.

Medieval Period

By the 9th century, the area now known as Bratislava became part of the Great Moravian Empire, the first major Slavic state in Central Europe. During this time, the settlement was known as Preslava. Great Moravia played an essential role in the spread of Christianity among the Slavic people, and it was likely during this period that Christian missionaries, including Cyril and Methodius, established their influence in the region, creating the first written Slavic alphabet.

After the fall of Great Moravia in the early 10th century, the area came under the control of the Hungarian Kingdom. The Hungarians fortified the settlement and began to establish the foundation of what would later become Bratislava. The first written mention of the city dates back to 907 AD in the Annals of the Bavarians, when the settlement was described as a border town within the Kingdom of Hungary. By the 11th century, Bratislava had begun to grow into an important market town and fortress.

In 1291, the town received its Magdeburg Rights, a set of privileges that granted it a high degree of autonomy. This period also saw the construction of the Bratislava Castle, which became a central fortress for the kingdom. Over the next few centuries, Bratislava continued to develop as a major commercial center, due to its advantageous position along the Danube River, which facilitated trade.

The Kingdom of Hungary and the Habsburg Dynasty

Bratislava's history took a major turn in the 16th century. In 1526, the Battle of Mohács saw the Ottoman Empire defeat the Hungarian army, leading to the division of Hungary between the Ottomans and the Habsburg Monarchy. With the Hungarian monarchy weakened, the Habsburgs took control of much of Hungary, and Bratislava began to emerge as an important center for the Habsburgs.

In 1536, the Coronation of Hungarian Kings moved to Bratislava following the fall of Buda (modern-day Budapest) to the Ottomans. For the next 300 years, Bratislava became the site of Royal Coronations, with many Hungarian kings crowned in the St. Martin's Cathedral. This was a period of growth for the city, which became an important administrative and religious center in Central Europe.

The 17th and 18th centuries saw significant cultural development in Bratislava as well, with the construction of numerous Baroque-style buildings and the rise of cultural institutions. However, the city also suffered from frequent conflicts, including wars with the Ottomans and other European powers.

The 19th Century: The Rise of Slovak Nationalism

The 19th century was a turning point in Bratislava's history, as it became a center for the rise of Slovak nationalism. During this period, the city saw the emergence of a growing Slovak identity that was distinct from Hungarian and Austrian influences. In 1848, Bratislava played a role in the Hungarian Revolution when the Slovaks, along with other ethnic groups in Hungary, sought greater autonomy and independence. Though the revolution ultimately failed, it marked the beginning of a more defined sense of Slovak national consciousness.

In the late 19th century, Bratislava was part of the Austro-Hungarian Empire, which had a lasting impact on the city's architecture and cultural landscape. The construction of new bridges over the Danube River, including the Apollo Bridge, and the growth of industrialization transformed the city into a modern urban center. Bratislava also became known as an important cultural hub, with many Slovak artists, writers, and intellectuals calling the city home.

20th Century: World Wars and Changing Borders

The 20th century brought dramatic changes to Bratislava, as Europe faced the turmoil of World War I and World War II. Following the collapse of the Austro-Hungarian Empire in 1918, Bratislava became part of the newly formed Czechoslovakia. The city, known as Pressburg at the time, was a prominent center of the Czechoslovak Republic, but the Slovak population struggled to assert its identity amidst the dominance of Czechs.

During World War II, Czechoslovakia was occupied by Nazi Germany, and the region saw the horrors of the war. After the war, Czechoslovakia became a communist state under Soviet influence, and Bratislava remained a significant part of the Eastern Bloc. The city, still under communist rule, saw significant industrialization but was also marked by political repression and limited freedoms.

In 1993, Czechoslovakia peacefully split into two independent countries — the Czech Republic and Slovakia. Bratislava became the capital of the new Slovak Republic, and with this new independence came a renewed sense of pride and purpose. Over the next few decades, Bratislava experienced rapid modernization, especially after the fall of communism, and it began to integrate into the European community.

Modern Bratislava

Today, Bratislava is a thriving European capital, known for its beautiful old town, its growing economy, and its cultural significance. The city has undergone a transformation in the past few decades, modernizing its infrastructure and expanding its international ties. However, it has managed to preserve much of its historical charm, with its medieval streets, ancient castles, and grand buildings still standing proudly as reminders of its past.

Bratislava's history has shaped it into a city that bridges the past and the future, combining the rich heritage of its past with the forward-thinking aspirations of the present. From its early days as a Celtic settlement to its current status as a modern European capital, Bratislava's story is one of resilience, reinvention, and a deep connection to its roots.

Whether you're strolling through its historical streets, visiting the iconic Bratislava Castle, or simply enjoying a coffee along the Danube, it's impossible not to feel the weight of history that surrounds this city. Bratislava's past is always present, and its future is being written one chapter at a time.

Why Visit Bratislava?

Why Visit Bratislava?

When I first set foot in Bratislava, I wasn't sure what to expect. It was a city that wasn't as famous as Prague or Budapest, but something about it seemed to beckon me. As soon as I arrived, I could tell this was a place with a distinct charm. Bratislava isn't a bustling metropolis like other European capitals, but that's exactly what makes it so special. It's small, easy to navigate, rich in history, and packed with character. If you're wondering whether Bratislava should be on your travel list, let me share exactly why I think it should be.

1. Compact and Walkable

One of the first things that stood out to me was how easy it was to explore the city on foot. Unlike many other European capitals that require hours of travel just to get from one part of the city to another, Bratislava is delightfully compact. The heart of the city is centered around the Old Town, which is a maze of cobbled streets, charming squares, and quaint alleys. You can easily walk from Bratislava Castle to the Old Town, passing by landmarks like St. Martin's Cathedral and the Primate's Palace along the way. It makes the whole experience feel personal and intimate, and you get to soak up the atmosphere without feeling rushed.

Bratislava's size makes it an ideal destination for a weekend getaway. You can explore the best parts of the city in a short amount of time, which allows you to really connect with the place rather than rushing through it.

2. A Rich Blend of History and Culture

Bratislava is steeped in history, and I could feel it the moment I arrived. The Bratislava Castle was my first stop, towering over the city with a view that stretches across the Danube River into neighboring Austria. Walking through the castle's courtyards, I couldn't help but imagine what life must have been like when it was a royal residence. The castle has witnessed centuries of history — from the Hungarian monarchy to the fall of the Austro-Hungarian Empire — and it holds a deep connection to the region's past.

The Old Town is like a living museum, with its medieval streets and buildings. Each one tells a story, from the St. Michael's Gate, one of the few remaining gates of the old city walls, to the Blue Church (Church of St. Elizabeth), with its striking blue tiles and delicate architecture. The Primate's Palace, with its beautiful Hall of Mirrors, and St. Martin's Cathedral, which once hosted Hungarian coronations, are must-sees that offer a tangible connection to centuries of royal and religious life.

But the history isn't just confined to grand landmarks. Even in the quieter corners of the city, like the Žižkova Street with its old houses, or the Bratislava City Museum, I found glimpses of the city's everyday history. The rich cultural tapestry was everywhere, whether in the architecture or the many museums dedicated to art, history, and even the communist era.

3. Affordable European Destination

Traveling around Europe can be expensive, but Bratislava offers fantastic value for money, especially when compared to other nearby cities like Vienna or Budapest. From accommodation to dining, everything is relatively affordable without compromising on quality. I found a cozy hotel in the city center that was just a short walk from all the attractions — and the price was a fraction of what I would have paid in other capitals. Even in restaurants and cafés, the prices were reasonable, with hearty Slovak meals and delicious local wines that didn't break the bank.

Bratislava is perfect for travelers who want to experience Europe without spending a fortune. Whether you're on a budget or willing to splurge a little, the city offers a variety of options for every wallet.

4. A Thriving Culinary Scene

When I visited Bratislava, I was eager to try the local food, and I was not disappointed. Slovak cuisine is hearty, comforting, and full of flavor. One of my favorite dishes was bryndzové halušky, a traditional Slovak dish made of potato dumplings covered in a creamy sheep's cheese sauce and topped with crispy bacon. It was delicious and filling — perfect after a day of sightseeing.

The city also has a thriving café culture. Many of the old cafés in the Old Town have a charming, nostalgic atmosphere, serving everything from coffee to pastries and local delicacies. The Café Mayer is one of the oldest cafés in the city, and I spent a lovely afternoon there, sipping coffee and watching the world go by. And if you're a fan of local wines, you'll find plenty of vineyards in the nearby Small Carpathian region, making it easy to sample the best Slovak wines in town.

For those who love trying local flavors, Bratislava is also known for its slivovica, a strong plum brandy, and various craft beers that are brewed locally. If you're looking for a taste of Slovakia, the city's food scene has it all.

5. A Blend of Old and New

What I found most fascinating about Bratislava was how the city combines the old and the new so seamlessly. While I wandered through the historic streets, I also found modern touches that gave the city a fresh, contemporary vibe. The UFO Observation Deck, atop the New Bridge, is a perfect example. It's a futuristic structure that offers one of the best panoramic views of the city. From there, you can see the contrast between the medieval Bratislava Castle and the more modern side of the city, with its skyscrapers and bustling commercial areas.

Bratislava has embraced modernity without losing its historical charm. It's a city that is constantly evolving — new restaurants, art galleries, and stylish cafés are popping up in the most unexpected places. The blend of the old-world charm with sleek, modern architecture gives the city a dynamic energy that I found incredibly appealing.

6. A Perfect Location for Day Trips

Bratislava's location makes it an ideal base for exploring the region. It sits at the borders of Austria, Hungary, and Slovakia, which means you can easily take day trips to neighboring countries. I was able to take a quick train ride to Vienna, just an hour away, to enjoy the grandeur of Austria's capital. Similarly, I could have easily visited Budapest or the Small Carpathians for a taste of the Slovak countryside. This proximity to other great European cities makes Bratislava an excellent starting point for exploring Central Europe.

7. Warm and Welcoming People

Perhaps the most memorable part of my visit was the people. I found the locals in Bratislava to be incredibly warm, friendly, and eager to share their city with visitors. From the moment I arrived, I was greeted with smiles and helpful advice. Whether it was a local shopkeeper recommending a great spot for lunch or a fellow traveler striking up a conversation about the best places to visit, I always felt welcomed.

Bratislava might not have the crowds that you'll find in other European capitals, but it more than makes up for it with its genuine warmth and hospitality.

Best Time to Visit Bratislava

Bratislava, Slovakia's charming capital, offers a unique experience year-round. But the best time to visit really depends on what kind of experience you're hoping for. Whether you're seeking vibrant festivals, pleasant weather for sightseeing, or a quiet escape, there's a perfect time for you to explore the city. Let me walk you through the different seasons in Bratislava, so you can choose the one that best suits your travel preferences.

Spring (March to May)

Spring is one of the best times to visit Bratislava. As the city begins to shake off the cold winter months, the weather becomes mild, and the city comes alive with blooming flowers and green spaces. Temperatures in spring range from about 10°C (50°F) to 17°C (63°F), making it a comfortable time to wander around the city and enjoy the outdoor sights.

During these months, Bratislava's Old Town is especially beautiful, as the flowers in Hlavné námestie (the main square) and the surrounding gardens start to bloom. The streets are a bit less crowded compared to the summer, which gives you a more peaceful experience while exploring.

Spring is also when various cultural festivals start to take place. One of the highlights is the Bratislava Music Festival, typically held in May, which features performances from local and international musicians. The city's concert halls and outdoor spaces come alive with classical music, jazz, and folk performances. It's an excellent time for culture lovers to visit, as the city bursts with artistic energy.

Summer (June to August)

Summer in Bratislava can be warm, with temperatures averaging between 20°C (68°F) and 28°C (82°F), but it can occasionally reach higher, especially in July and August. The warm weather makes this an ideal time for outdoor activities along the Danube River, where you can take a boat tour or even hop on a river cruise to nearby destinations like Vienna or Budapest. The city's parks, like Medická Záhrada or Sad Janka Kráľa, are perfect for picnics, and the riverbanks are lined with people enjoying the sunshine.

Bratislava's outdoor cafes and terraces are another big draw during the summer months. I loved spending afternoons sipping coffee or trying a local craft beer while watching the world go by. The weather is perfect for enjoying the UFO Observation Deck on the New Bridge, which offers stunning views of the city and the river.

However, summer is also the most popular time for tourists, which means the city can feel busier, especially around well-known sites like the Bratislava Castle or the Old Town. If you don't mind the crowds, summer festivals are in full swing. The Bratislava Old Town Festival in June is a celebration of local crafts, food, and music, with various performances taking place across the city. It's a great time to immerse yourself in the local culture, though be prepared for larger crowds.

Autumn (September to November)

Autumn is another fantastic time to visit Bratislava. The weather is still mild in September and October, with temperatures ranging from 12°C (54°F) to 19°C (66°F), making it perfect for outdoor activities. The city's parks and gardens take on a golden hue as the fall leaves change color, creating a picturesque setting for a walk through the Old Town or a hike up to Bratislava Castle for a view of the city bathed in autumn light.

Autumn also marks the harvest season, so it's an ideal time to explore the nearby Small Carpathian wine region. Bratislava is surrounded by vineyards, and during the fall months, the local wineries offer wine-tasting tours and festivals celebrating the harvest. If you're a wine lover, this is an experience not to be missed, as you can sample some of the finest local wines while soaking in the autumn landscape. The Bratislava Wine Festival, typically held in September, is a particularly popular event for wine enthusiasts.

Additionally, autumn brings fewer tourists compared to the summer, so it's a great time for a more relaxed and quieter experience. The city is still lively, but you can enjoy the attractions without the large crowds, especially at places like the Primate's Palace or St. Martin's Cathedral.

Winter (December to February)

Winter in Bratislava can be cold, with temperatures often dipping below 0°C (32°F), especially in January and February. Snow is not uncommon, and when it does fall, the city takes on a magical, fairytale-like atmosphere. The chilly weather means you might not be spending as much time outdoors, but the beauty of the city in winter is undeniable. The Bratislava Castle and the Old Town are particularly charming when dusted with snow, and you can enjoy the city's stunning Christmas lights and decorations.

Bratislava is famous for its Christmas markets, which are held from late November through December. These markets are a major highlight for anyone visiting during the winter months. I visited the Old Town Christmas Market in December, and the entire area was transformed into a winter wonderland. The smell of mulled wine, roasted chestnuts, and Slovak holiday treats filled the air, while festive music played from every corner. It's a wonderful way to experience the Slovak culture and traditions during the holiday season.

If you're visiting Bratislava in winter, be sure to try a warm cup of slivovica, the local plum brandy, or enjoy a hearty bowl of kapustnica (a sour cabbage soup), a Slovak winter specialty. The cold weather makes it the perfect season for indulging in warm, comforting food.

Winter is also the least crowded time of year for tourists, so it's ideal if you prefer a more peaceful visit. You can enjoy the sights and attractions at your own pace, without the crowds that come during peak travel seasons.

Chapter 2. Planning Your Trip

Visa and Travel Requirements

Visa and Travel Requirements for Bratislava

Bratislava, the capital of Slovakia, is a member of the European Union (EU) and the Schengen Area. Whether or not you need a visa depends on your nationality and the country you are coming from. Slovakia follows the EU's regulations on border controls, so the visa and travel requirements are largely in line with other Schengen Area countries.

Here's a detailed look at the visa and travel requirements when planning a trip to Bratislava:

---

1. Citizens of the European Union (EU) and European Economic Area (EEA)

If you are a citizen of any EU country (like Germany, France, Italy, Spain, etc.) or a European Economic Area (EEA) member state, you do not need a visa to travel to Slovakia. Similarly, citizens of Switzerland can enter Slovakia without a visa.

As an EU or EEA citizen:

- You can enter Slovakia with just your national ID card or passport.
- There are no restrictions on your stay, and you can live, work, or study in Slovakia without the need for a special residence permit.

2. Citizens of Switzerland

Switzerland is not an EU member but is part of the Schengen Area. Therefore, Swiss citizens do not need a visa to visit Slovakia. A valid Swiss passport or national ID card is sufficient for entry.

3. Citizens of Schengen Area Countries

Slovakia is a member of the Schengen Area, so citizens of other Schengen Zone countries can freely travel to Bratislava without needing a visa. Citizens of the Schengen Zone only need to show their national ID card at border crossings or airports.

Schengen Area countries include:

- Austria
- Belgium
- Czech Republic
- Estonia
- Finland
- France
- Germany

- Greece
- Hungary
- Iceland
- Italy
- Latvia
- Lithuania
- Luxembourg
- Malta
- Netherlands
- Norway
- Poland
- Portugal
- Slovakia
- Slovenia
- Spain
- Sweden
- Switzerland

4. Citizens of Non-Schengen EU Countries

Some countries in the EU are not part of the Schengen Area. These countries include Bulgaria, Croatia, Cyprus, and Romania. Citizens of these countries can travel to Slovakia without a visa if they are traveling for short stays of up to 90 days.

- Citizens of Bulgaria, Croatia, Cyprus, and Romania can use their national passports or identity cards for entry.

5. Citizens of Non-EU Countries (Visa Requirements)

If you are from a non-EU country that is not part of the Schengen Area, you will need to check whether you require a Schengen Visa to visit Bratislava and Slovakia.

Slovakia, as a Schengen member, follows the same visa policies as other Schengen countries. The Schengen Visa allows you to visit Slovakia as well as any other Schengen member state within a 90-day period during a 180-day timeframe.

Schengen Visa (Short Stay Visa)

- Who needs it? Citizens of countries that do not have a Schengen Visa Waiver Agreement with the European Union will need a Schengen Visa to visit Slovakia.
  These include citizens from countries like:
  1. India
  2. Russia
  3. China
  4. United States (only for long stays or if traveling for specific reasons, like business)
  5. Nigeria
  6. Indonesia

7. South Africa
  8. Philippines
  9. Several countries in the Middle East (e.g., Saudi Arabia, UAE)
- Types of Schengen Visa:
  1. Short-stay visa (type C) – for stays up to 90 days within a 180-day period. This is the most common visa for tourism and business trips.
  2. Multiple-entry visa – if you plan to visit multiple Schengen countries during your trip.

Travel Passes for Bratislava

While the topic of visa and travel requirements is crucial, many travelers also want to make sure they are getting the most convenient options for exploring Bratislava once they arrive. Some travel passes can simplify your visit and provide access to public transportation, museums, and popular attractions at discounted rates.

The Bratislava Card is one such pass, and it offers:

- Free public transport around the city
- Free or discounted entry to over 10 museums and attractions
- Discounts on other services, such as river cruises and local shops

However, this pass is only available for tourists, and you should check if it suits your travel needs before purchasing.

Currency and Customs

Currency, Language, and Customs in Bratislava

When traveling to a new city, understanding the local currency, language, and customs is essential for a smooth and respectful experience. In Bratislava, Slovakia's charming capital, these elements are intertwined with rich Slovak traditions, European influences, and practical considerations for travelers. Let's dive into what you need to know about currency, language, and customs in this beautiful city.

Currency: The Euro (€)

Since Slovakia became a member of the European Union in 2004, it adopted the Euro (€) as its official currency in 2009. This makes Bratislava very convenient for travelers coming from other Eurozone countries. If you're coming from a non-Eurozone country, this simplifies your travel, as you won't need to worry about currency exchange fees in the city.

- Cash and Cards: The Euro is the currency used for all transactions in Bratislava. While credit and debit cards are widely accepted in most restaurants, shops, and hotels, it's still a good idea to carry some cash for smaller purchases, such as snacks, souvenirs, or tips. Cash is also essential for local markets, street vendors, or smaller establishments, where cards may not be accepted.

- ATMs and Currency Exchange: ATMs are abundant in the city, and you'll find them in most central locations, including near major tourist spots. Currency exchange offices are also readily available, especially around the Old Town and near popular tourist attractions. Most exchange offices are open during regular business hours, though rates can vary, so it's a good idea to shop around.

- Tips: While tipping isn't mandatory, it's common to leave a 10-15% tip in restaurants if you're satisfied with the service. In cafes or bars, rounding up the bill or leaving small change is also appreciated. Taxi drivers usually expect a 5-10% tip, depending on the service provided.

Customs and Etiquette in Bratislava

Slovak culture is characterized by a blend of traditional values and modern European influences. As with any travel destination, understanding local customs and social etiquette will make your visit more enjoyable and respectful. Here's what to expect when interacting with locals in Bratislava:

1. Greetings and Social Etiquette:

- Handshakes: When meeting someone for the first time or in formal settings, a firm handshake is customary. It's polite to greet the other person with their title (Mr., Mrs.) and surname. In more casual settings, "Ahoj" (Hello) or "Čau" (Hi) can be used among friends and acquaintances.
- Personal Space: Slovaks value personal space in public, and they generally maintain a comfortable distance when talking to others. Don't be surprised if people keep a polite distance, particularly in professional or formal interactions.
- Titles and Formality: It's common to use formal titles in Slovakia until you're invited to use first names, especially when meeting people for the first time. Addressing someone by their last name or Mr./Mrs. + surname is a sign of respect
- Eye Contact: Maintaining good eye contact during conversation is important in Slovakia. It is considered respectful and shows interest in the conversation.

2. Dining Etiquette:

Slovaks are known for their hospitality, and when dining out or visiting someone's home, there are a few things to keep in mind:

- Invitations: If you're invited to a Slovak home, it's polite to bring a small gift, such as a bottle of wine, flowers, or chocolates. This gesture shows appreciation for their hospitality.
- Starting the Meal: It's customary to wait for the host to begin eating before you start your meal. Saying "Na zdravie" (Cheers) before taking a sip of your drink is common in social settings.
- Table Manners: Keep your hands visible (resting on the table, not in your lap) during the meal, and always use utensils when eating, even for foods like pizza or sandwiches. It's considered rude to eat with your hands in a formal setting.
- Tipping: In restaurants, leaving a 10-15% tip is appreciated if the service is good. However, tipping is not mandatory, and the amount you leave is up to your discretion. It's common to leave the tip in cash, even if you pay the bill by card.

3. Punctuality and Time:

Punctuality is valued in Slovakia, especially in professional or formal settings. Being on time for meetings, appointments, or social events is considered respectful. If you're running late, it's polite to notify the person you're meeting.

- Business Etiquette: Slovakia's business culture can be quite formal. Handshakes, direct eye contact, and professional attire are important during business meetings. Small talk is common at the beginning of meetings, and it's often polite to discuss topics like the weather, sports, or current events.

4. Public Behavior and Customs:

- Quiet and Reserved: Slovaks tend to be more reserved compared to people in some other European countries. Public displays of affection are not as common, and loud behavior in public places is frowned upon.

- Respect for Tradition: Slovakia has a deep respect for its cultural traditions, especially when it comes to national holidays, religious observances, and family events. If you're in Bratislava during a significant Slovak holiday, such as Christmas or Easter, expect to see the local community engaged in traditional celebrations and festivities. These events can be a wonderful opportunity for visitors to experience Slovak customs and cuisine.

5. Dress Code:

In general, Slovaks dress smartly and have a good sense of personal style. For a casual day out, you'll find that people wear modern, comfortable clothing, but it's also not uncommon to see individuals in more formal or elegant attire when attending cultural events, restaurants, or business meetings. Dressing appropriately for the occasion shows respect for Slovak culture.

Chapter 3. Getting There

By Air: Bratislava Airport

By Air: Bratislava Airport – M. R. Štefánik International Airport (BTS)

When traveling to Bratislava, the most convenient entry point by air is M. R. Štefánik International Airport (BTS), also known as Bratislava Airport. Located approximately 9 kilometers (5.5 miles) from the city center, the airport offers easy access to the city via taxi, shuttle services, and public transport. It is the main gateway for international flights into Slovakia and serves as an important hub for travelers heading to Bratislava and the surrounding regions.

Overview of Bratislava Airport

M. R. Štefánik International Airport (BTS) is named after Milan Rastislav Štefánik, a Slovak politician, aviator, and general. The airport is the largest in Slovakia and plays a vital role in connecting the country to international destinations. Although smaller compared to airports in larger European cities, it is a modern and efficient airport that handles both domestic and international flights.

The airport serves a range of airlines, from low-cost carriers like Ryanair and Wizz Air to full-service airlines. It's a particularly popular entry point for travelers coming from nearby countries such as Austria, Hungary, and Czech Republic.

Terminals at Bratislava Airport

Bratislava Airport consists of one main terminal that is divided into two sections: Terminal 1 (international flights) and Terminal 2 (primarily for Schengen area flights). Here's a closer look at each terminal:

Terminal 1: International Flights

Terminal 1 handles most of the international flights, including those to non-Schengen countries. This is the terminal you'll use if you're arriving from destinations like the United Kingdom, Russia, or Israel.

- Services & Facilities:
    - Duty-free shops offering cosmetics, alcohol, tobacco, and Slovak souvenirs
    - Currency exchange and ATMs
    - Cafés and restaurants serving Slovak and international cuisine
    - Free Wi-Fi available throughout the terminal
    - Information desks to assist with flight information and local transport
    - Car rental desks (for picking up vehicles upon arrival)
    - Lounges for business class travelers or those seeking additional comfort

Terminal 2: Schengen Flights

Terminal 2 handles flights within the Schengen Area. Flights from countries like Austria, Germany, Czech Republic, and Italy typically arrive and depart from this terminal. It's more streamlined in terms of amenities but still provides the essential services.

- Services & Facilities:
    - Smaller duty-free shops and retail outlets
    - Cafés offering snacks and drinks
    - Currency exchange services
    - Free Wi-Fi and charging stations
    - Basic seating areas with ample space for passengers waiting for their flights

Cost of Flights to Bratislava Airport

The cost of flying into Bratislava Airport depends on a variety of factors such as the airline, the time of booking, and the season. For example, low-cost carriers like Ryanair and Wizz Air frequently offer budget-friendly options to and from Bratislava, especially if you book in advance.

- From major European cities:
    - Flights from London (Luton) to Bratislava can range from €15-€60 one way, depending on how early you book and the season.
    - A flight from Vienna to Bratislava (just an hour's drive away) might be as low as €20-€30, though flights between these cities are less frequent.
    - From Berlin, a one-way ticket may range from €25-€80 with budget airlines.
- Peak season vs. Off-season:
    - Summer months (June-August) generally see higher prices, especially with airlines offering flights to vacation destinations. Expect prices to rise during holidays and special events in Slovakia.
    - In contrast, during the low season (fall and winter months), budget flights can be as low as €10-€40 for one-way tickets from nearby cities.

Typical Costs for Airport Services:

- Taxi to the city center: A taxi ride from Bratislava Airport to the city center typically costs between €15-€25, depending on traffic and your destination within the city.
- Public transportation: The bus (Lines 61 and N61) runs directly to the city center and costs around €0.90 for a one-way ticket. It's a budget-friendly option, though it may take a bit longer than a taxi.
- Airport Shuttle: Many shuttle services are available from the airport to different areas in the city. Prices typically range from €5-€10 per person for a shared ride, though private shuttles may cost more.

Travel Tips for Flying into Bratislava

- Public transport options: If you're traveling on a budget, take advantage of public transportation, as buses from the airport to the city center are efficient and inexpensive. The bus line 61 runs regularly and offers a good connection to the city center and the main train station.

- Airport transfers: For more comfort and convenience, consider pre-booking an airport transfer or shuttle. Some hotels also offer free shuttle services from the airport to their properties, so check with your accommodation in advance.

- Arrival procedures: Expect relatively quick and smooth arrival procedures, as the airport is not as large or crowded as major international airports. You'll typically pass through passport control (if you're arriving from a non-Schengen country) or customs if necessary.

By Train: Rail Connections to Major Cities

By Train: Rail Connections to Major Cities, Terminals, and Costs

Traveling to Bratislava by train is not only an easy and convenient option but also one that allows you to enjoy the beautiful scenic views of the European countryside. Slovakia has well-established rail connections that link Bratislava with major cities in Austria, Hungary, the Czech Republic, and other neighboring countries, making it a great choice for international travelers as well as those coming from within Slovakia.

Major Rail Connections to Bratislava

Bratislava's Main Railway Station (Bratislava Hlavná stanica) serves as the central hub for both domestic and international train services. The station connects the city to several major European destinations, providing quick and comfortable travel options for visitors arriving from nearby cities and countries.

1. From Vienna (Austria)

One of the most popular international train routes to Bratislava is the Vienna to Bratislava connection. The two cities are just about 60 kilometers (37 miles) apart, making for a quick and convenient train ride.

- Train options: Trains from Vienna typically operate on a frequent basis, with both InterCity (IC) and Regional Express (RE) trains making the journey.
- Duration: The ride takes about 1 hour.
- Cost: A one-way ticket typically costs between €10 to €15, depending on the time and class of service (standard or first class).
- Frequency: Trains run approximately every 30 minutes throughout the day, offering great flexibility for travelers.

2. From Budapest (Hungary)

Trains from Budapest to Bratislava are also very popular, connecting Hungary's capital with the Slovakian capital in a relatively short time.

- Train options: The EuroCity (EC) and InterCity (IC) trains are available for this route, providing a comfortable and fast way to travel.
- Duration: The train ride between Budapest and Bratislava usually takes around 2.5 to 3 hours.

- Cost: Tickets generally range from €15 to €30, depending on the class and time of booking.
- Frequency: Several trains run daily, providing plenty of options for travelers.

3. From Prague (Czech Republic)

Traveling by train from Prague to Bratislava is a great option for those visiting the Czech Republic. The journey is comfortable, with scenic views of the countryside.

- Train options: The EuroCity (EC) and InterCity (IC) trains are available for this route as well, and they offer both standard and first-class seating.
- Duration: The ride takes approximately 4 to 4.5 hours.
- Cost: A one-way ticket can range from €20 to €40, depending on the time of day, class, and how far in advance the ticket is purchased.
- Frequency: Trains run multiple times a day, making it easy to find a convenient time to travel.

4. From Krakow (Poland)

For travelers coming from Krakow, Poland, there are direct trains to Bratislava, although this route may not be as frequent as the others. It is a great choice for those exploring Eastern Europe.

- Train options: The EuroCity (EC) trains connect Krakow to Bratislava.
- Duration: The journey takes about 7 hours.
- Cost: Tickets range from €25 to €45, depending on the class of service and ticket availability.
- Frequency: Trains are less frequent on this route, with one or two direct trains available daily.

Terminals: Bratislava Main Railway Station

The central station in Bratislava is called Bratislava Hlavná stanica (Bratislava Main Railway Station). It is the largest and busiest railway station in Slovakia, handling both domestic and international connections.

Overview of Bratislava Hlavná Stanica:

- Location: The station is located about 2 kilometers (1.2 miles) from the city center, and it is easily accessible by public transportation, including trams, buses, and taxis.
- Facilities:
    - Ticket offices and self-service machines for purchasing tickets.
    - Waiting areas with seating and basic amenities.
    - Shops, including a supermarket, small stores, and snack bars.
    - Cafés and restaurants for travelers to enjoy a bite before or after their journey.
    - Luggage storage services for those who need to store their bags for a short while.
    - Currency exchange and ATMs available for international visitors.
- Public Transport Connections: Once you arrive at the station, there are several options for getting to the city center:
    - Trams: Tram lines 1, 2, and 3 connect the station to the Old Town and other parts of Bratislava.

- Buses: Bus lines also serve the station, with frequent connections to the city center and nearby areas.
- Taxis: Taxis are readily available outside the station, and the ride to the center of town takes about 10 minutes.

Ticket Prices and Travel Tips

- Ticket Prices: The cost of tickets for international trains is typically determined by the distance and the type of service. It's often cheaper to book tickets in advance, especially for popular routes like Vienna to Bratislava or Budapest to Bratislava.
    - Domestic Train (Bratislava to other Slovak cities): Tickets are generally €5 to €15 for a one-way ticket, depending on the distance and class.
    - International Train: As noted earlier, prices range from €10 to €45, depending on the route, time of booking, and class of service.
- Booking Tickets: Tickets can be purchased at the ticket office at Bratislava Main Railway Station, from self-service kiosks, or online through the official Slovak Railways website or apps like Omio or Trainline. For international routes, it's often best to book ahead to secure the best prices and seat availability.
- Travel Passes: If you plan on traveling extensively by train, consider purchasing a Eurail Pass or Interrail Pass, which provides unlimited travel within Slovakia and other European countries for a set number of days. These passes are ideal for tourists who plan on exploring multiple destinations by train.

Advantages of Traveling by Train to Bratislava

- Scenic Routes: One of the great advantages of traveling by train to Bratislava is the scenic journey. Whether you're traveling from Vienna, Budapest, or Prague, the views from the train windows offer picturesque landscapes, picturesque towns, and the beauty of the Danube River.
- Comfortable and Relaxing: Trains in Slovakia and neighboring countries offer comfortable seating, ample legroom, and clean facilities, making it a relaxing option compared to buses or cars. The option to walk around, visit the restaurant car, or simply stretch your legs is also a great benefit.
- No Airport Hassles: Train travel eliminates the need for airport security checks, long lines, and the need to arrive hours in advance, which can make it a faster and less stressful option for short distances

By Bus and Car: Transportation Options

By Bus and Car: Transportation Options to Bratislava, Terminals, and Costs

When planning your trip to Bratislava, there are excellent bus and car travel options available that allow you to experience the flexibility and affordability of getting to this charming European capital. Whether you're coming from neighboring cities or even further abroad, both bus and car travel offer practical and scenic routes into the city. Below, we'll dive into these two transportation methods, covering everything from bus terminals and car rentals to typical costs and travel tips.

By Bus: Convenient and Affordable Travel to Bratislava

Bratislava is well-connected to various European cities by bus. It is one of the most budget-friendly options for travelers, especially those coming from nearby countries like Austria, Hungary, Czech Republic, and Germany. Buses offer direct routes to Bratislava from major cities, providing an accessible and cost-effective way to get to the Slovakian capital.

Major Bus Routes to Bratislava:

1. From Vienna (Austria):
    - Duration: A bus from Vienna to Bratislava typically takes about 1 to 1.5 hours, making it a convenient option for travelers heading to Bratislava from Austria's capital.
    - Cost: One-way tickets can cost between €5 to €12, depending on the bus company and how far in advance the ticket is purchased. Budget bus companies like FlixBus often offer the lowest rates.
    - Frequency: Buses run regularly throughout the day, with departures every 30 minutes to an hour. During peak travel times, this frequency increases, ensuring flexibility for travelers.
2. From Budapest (Hungary):
    - Duration: The bus ride from Budapest to Bratislava generally takes around 3 to 3.5 hours.
    - Cost: One-way fares range from €10 to €20, depending on the bus operator and booking time.
    - Frequency: Several buses operate on this route daily, giving travelers plenty of options.
3. From Prague (Czech Republic):
    - Duration: A bus from Prague to Bratislava typically takes 4.5 to 5 hours.
    - Cost: Fares usually range from €15 to €30, depending on the bus company and booking conditions.
    - Frequency: Buses run multiple times a day, and services are often provided by companies like FlixBus or RegioJet.
4. From Other Cities in Europe:
    - Germany, Poland, Croatia, and other European cities are also well-connected to Bratislava by long-distance bus services. The prices and travel durations vary but remain affordable compared to other modes of transport, such as trains or flights.

Bus Terminals in Bratislava

Once you arrive by bus in Bratislava, you'll likely disembark at one of the city's major bus stations, where you can easily find your way to the city center.

1. **Bratislava Nivy Bus Station:**
    - Location: Bratislava Nivy Bus Station is the main and most modern bus terminal in the city, located about 3 km (2 miles) from the city center. It is well-connected to public transport, making it easy for visitors to reach Old Town and other popular destinations.
    - Facilities: The station offers a range of amenities, including restaurants, shops, luggage storage, and currency exchange services. There's also a large mall in the same building, offering various retail outlets and food options for travelers.
    - Public transport: The bus station is served by tram and bus lines that will take you to the Old Town (just a short ride away) and other central locations. The ride to the city center typically takes around 10-15 minutes.
2. **Mlynské Nivy Bus Terminal:**
    - This station also serves various regional routes, and buses arriving from cities like Vienna, Budapest, or Prague may stop here.
    - The terminal is close to major transport links, including taxis, buses, and trams.

By Car: Freedom and Flexibility to Explore Bratislava

Driving to Bratislava by car is a fantastic option for travelers who enjoy the freedom to explore at their own pace and potentially visit other cities along the way. With Bratislava's proximity to neighboring countries like Austria, Hungary, and the Czech Republic, the city is well-connected by highways and motorways.

Driving to Bratislava from Neighboring Cities:

1. **From Vienna (Austria):**
    - Duration: If you're driving from Vienna to Bratislava, the journey takes about 45 minutes to 1 hour. The two cities are only 60 kilometers (37 miles) apart, so the drive is quick and scenic.
    - Route: The A4 motorway connects Vienna to Bratislava, making the drive straightforward. Ensure you have a vignette (toll sticker) for Austrian highways if you're traveling by car in Austria.
2. **From Budapest (Hungary):**
    - Duration: Driving from Budapest to Bratislava takes about 2.5 to 3 hours, depending on traffic and the route taken.
    - Route: The most direct route is via the M1 motorway and E575, which takes you through towns and countryside along the way. It's a smooth and easy drive, offering a chance to enjoy the Hungarian and Slovak landscapes.
3. **From Prague (Czech Republic):**
    - Duration: The drive from Prague to Bratislava usually takes around 3.5 to 4 hours.
    - Route: The D1 motorway and E65 take you from Prague through Slovakia's countryside to Bratislava, making it an efficient route.

Cost of Driving to Bratislava:

- Fuel: The cost of fuel will vary depending on the type of vehicle you're driving and the route you take. On average, expect to pay €1.30 to €1.50 per liter of petrol or diesel in both Austria and Slovakia.
    - For example, the Vienna to Bratislava journey (around 60 kilometers) would cost approximately €6 to €10 in fuel, depending on your car's fuel efficiency.
- Tolls and Vignettes:
    - Austria: If you're driving through Austria, you'll need to purchase a vignette (toll sticker) for driving on motorways. A 10-day vignette for a car costs about €9.
    - Slovakia: Slovakia has a similar system for its motorways. You'll need a vignette for highways, which costs about €10 for 10 days.
- Car Rental: If you're renting a car, expect to pay an average of €25 to €50 per day for a basic economy car. Prices can fluctuate depending on the rental company, the season, and how far in advance you book.

Parking in Bratislava:

Once you arrive in Bratislava, finding parking can be straightforward in central areas, though some spots may require you to pay. There are several paid parking zones throughout the city, especially near the Old Town and popular tourist attractions.

- Public Parking: Many areas have designated parking meters, and you can expect to pay around €1 to €2 per hour for parking.
- Private Parking: Hotels and some shopping centers offer secure parking for guests, but it's often more expensive than public options. Rates can range from €10 to €20 per day.

Chapter 4. Getting Around

Trams

Getting Around Bratislava by Tram: A Convenient and Scenic Option

Trams are one of the most popular and efficient modes of public transportation in Bratislava. The city boasts an extensive tram network, offering visitors and locals an easy way to explore various parts of the city, including the Old Town, Bratislava Castle, and other key attractions. With frequent services, reasonable fares, and an eco-friendly impact, traveling by tram in Bratislava is both practical and pleasant.

Trams in Bratislava: Overview and Routes

The Bratislava tram system is operated by DPB (Dopravný podnik Bratislava), the city's public transport company. It covers a significant portion of the city and connects neighborhoods, commercial areas, and tourist attractions. The trams run throughout the day, with frequent stops near most key areas, making them an excellent way to get around the city quickly and comfortably.

Tram Routes:

There are several tram lines operating in Bratislava, each serving different districts and offering connections to important sites. Some of the main tram lines include:

1. Tram Line 1: This line connects Hlavná stanica (the main train station) to the Old Town, offering a direct route through key areas of the city. It's an excellent line for visitors as it passes through major attractions like Slovenské národné múzeum (Slovak National Museum) and Špitálska Street.
2. Tram Line 2: This route runs from Petržalka (the southern district) to the Old Town and then through to Nové Mesto. It's ideal for those traveling from residential neighborhoods to the city center.
3. Tram Line 4: Another important line that connects areas like Kramáre to Old Town and passes through cultural spots like Bratislava's Central Market.
4. Tram Line 8: Serving areas like ZOO (Bratislava Zoo) and Kráľovské údolie, this line is especially helpful for those visiting recreational and green spaces.

Tram Terminals and Stops

The tram network is well-connected, with several key terminals and main stops scattered across the city, making it easy to hop on and off throughout your travels. Some of the important tram terminals in Bratislava include:

1. Hlavná Stanica (Main Train Station):

- Located in the city center, Hlavná Stanica is one of the busiest transport hubs in Bratislava, offering connections to both trams and buses. This station provides easy access to the Old Town and other major areas of the city.
2. Špitálska:
    - This stop is located near the Slovak National Museum and provides good access to the surrounding historical district and several key shopping areas.
3. Old Town (Staré Mesto):
    - Several tram lines pass through Old Town with stops such as Most SNP (Bridge of the Slovak National Uprising) and Hurbanovo námestie. These stops are perfect for those who want to explore the historic heart of Bratislava.
4. Petržalka:
    - This is one of the largest residential areas of Bratislava and connects to the city center via several tram lines. The Petržalka tram stop is ideal for reaching the southern parts of the city.
5. ZOO (Bratislava Zoo):
    - If you're looking to visit the Bratislava Zoo, taking tram line 8 will bring you close to the Kráľovské údolie area.

Tram Ticket Prices and Costs

The ticket system for trams in Bratislava is integrated with other forms of public transport, including buses and trolleybuses. The prices are relatively affordable, and tickets are valid for all forms of public transport within the designated zones.

Ticket Types and Costs:

1. Single Ticket (30 minutes):
    - Cost: €0.90
    - This ticket allows you to travel for 30 minutes on any tram (or bus/trolleybus) within the city limits.
2. Single Ticket (60 minutes):
    - Cost: €1.20
    - This ticket gives you 60 minutes of travel time, which is perfect if you plan to change trams or other public transport during your journey.
3. Short-Term Pass (90 minutes):
    - Cost: €1.50
    - Ideal for tourists who may need extra time to explore or hop between different stops in the city.
4. Day Pass
    - Cost: €4.50
    - If you're planning to explore the city extensively, this is a cost-effective option, giving you unlimited travel on trams, buses, and trolleybuses for 24 hours.
5. Three-Day Pass:
    - Cost: €13.50

- For those staying in the city for a longer time, the three-day pass offers unlimited travel across the city on trams and other public transport.

How to Buy Tickets:

- Ticket Machines: You can purchase tickets from ticket machines located at major tram stations or stops.
- SMS Tickets: A convenient option is buying your ticket through a mobile app or SMS, which you can use to validate your ride before boarding.
- Onboard Purchase: Some trams offer onboard ticket purchases, but it's recommended to buy your ticket beforehand to avoid paying a higher fare (the onboard tickets usually cost slightly more).

Tram Operating Hours

Trams in Bratislava generally operate from 4:30 AM until 11:30 PM, with some extended services on weekends or public holidays. The trams are a reliable way to get around, though for late-night travel, it's better to opt for night buses as the trams stop operating around midnight.

Advantages of Traveling by Tram in Bratislava

1. Affordability: Tram fares are among the most budget-friendly options for getting around the city, especially for short trips or tourists who need to make several stops during their day.

2. Environmental Impact: Trams are one of the eco-friendliest transportation options in the city, helping reduce the carbon footprint of daily commutes.

3. Convenience: With regular services, trams make it easy to navigate through Bratislava, whether you're traveling from the train station to the Old Town or heading to Bratislava Castle.

4. Scenic Routes: Trams offer great views of the city, especially along routes passing through areas like Petržalka, Old Town, and near the Danube River.

Buses

Getting Around Bratislava by Bus: Efficient and Affordable Travel

Buses in Bratislava offer a convenient and affordable way to navigate the city, especially for reaching areas that aren't directly serviced by trams or trolleybuses. Whether you're heading from Bratislava's Old Town to the suburbs or making your way to popular shopping centers or parks, the extensive bus network covers much of the city and beyond, making it an essential part of the city's public transport system.

Buses in Bratislava: Overview and Routes

The Bratislava Bus System is operated by DPB (Dopravný podnik Bratislava), the same company that handles trams and trolleybuses. With over 50 bus routes, the network connects key residential districts, commercial areas, and tourist spots, making it a practical choice for those looking to explore the city.

Main Bus Routes:

- Line 50: One of the primary routes in Bratislava, it connects central areas to Petržalka, the city's largest residential district, and further to Rajka, Hungary. This line is ideal for those traveling across the Danube River or exploring the city's southern districts.
- Line 29: A key line that travels from Hlavná Stanica (the main train station) to Nové Mesto, passing through the Slovak National Museum and popular shopping centers.
- Line 23: Connecting the city center with Kramáre, this route is essential for reaching areas like Bratislava Zoo and National Football Stadium.
- Line 84: This line connects Bratislava's airport with the city center, allowing easy access for travelers coming into or leaving the city.

Bus Terminals and Major Stops in Bratislava

Bratislava's bus system includes several important terminals and key stops, allowing easy access to various parts of the city. These stations are typically located near train stations, shopping centers, and tourist attractions, making it easy for visitors to catch a bus to their destination.

Major Bus Terminals:

1. Bratislava Nivy Bus Station:
    - Location: This is the main bus terminal in Bratislava, located about 3 km (2 miles) from the city center. It serves as a hub for long-distance buses coming from Austria, Hungary, and Czech Republic, among others.
    - Facilities: The terminal has a modern building with shops, restaurants, and waiting areas. It is well-connected to the city center via tram and bus routes. Visitors can easily take tram lines to reach popular tourist spots like the Old Town or Bratislava Castle.
    - Public Transport Connections: Multiple tram and bus lines, such as Lines 202, 205, and 93, offer easy access to the city's main attractions.
2. Mlynské Nivy Bus Terminal:
    - Located near the city center, this terminal serves regional and international bus services, making it convenient for those traveling from Bratislava's surrounding areas or nearby countries.
    - Public Transport: It is connected to other parts of the city by trams and buses, and it offers easy access to business districts and shopping malls.
3. Hlavná Stanica (Main Train Station):
    - Located close to the city center, Hlavná Stanica is the primary railway station in Bratislava. It is also a major bus hub, where you'll find buses connecting to the train station and surrounding areas.

- Bus Connections: Lines 50 and 29 depart from here, connecting to various destinations around the city.
4. Airport Bus Terminal:
    - Located at M. R. Štefánik Airport, the Airport Bus Terminal provides connections between the airport and the city center, including bus line 84, which directly links the airport with central Bratislava.
    - This terminal is ideal for travelers coming into the city and needing quick access to their hotel or other destinations.

Bus Ticket Prices and Costs in Bratislava

Bratislava's bus system uses the same ticketing system as its trams and trolleybuses, making it easy for passengers to switch between modes of transport. Tickets are reasonably priced and can be purchased from ticket machines, onboard, or via SMS.

Ticket Types and Costs:

1. Single Ticket (30 minutes):
    - Cost: €0.90
    - This allows 30 minutes of travel across the city, covering buses, trams, and trolleybuses. It's a perfect option for short trips or when you need to change buses or trams within the city.
2. Single Ticket (60 minutes):
    - Cost: €1.20
    - For longer journeys or those making multiple stops, this ticket is valid for 60 minutes of travel, giving you enough time to get from one side of the city to another.
3. Short-Term Pass (90 minutes):
    - Cost: €1.50
    - This ticket is perfect for tourists who might need a little extra time to explore or make connections across the city.
4. Day Pass:
    - Cost: €4.50
    - If you plan to explore Bratislava throughout the day, a 24-hour pass allows unlimited travel on buses, trams, and trolleybuses, making it an excellent choice for tourists.
5. Three-Day Pass:
    - Cost: €13.50
    - For longer stays, this pass allows unlimited travel within the city for three consecutive days. It's ideal for those who want to thoroughly explore Bratislava without worrying about individual fares.
6. Group Tickets:
    - Cost: €3.50 (for up to 5 people)
    - A group ticket allows up to five people to travel together for 90 minutes.

Ticket Purchase Options:

- Ticket Machines: You can buy tickets from self-service machines at tram and bus stations.
- SMS Tickets: Another convenient way to purchase tickets is through the Slovak Public Transport mobile app or via SMS, which are activated upon purchase.
- Onboard Purchase: In some cases, passengers can buy tickets directly from the driver on the bus, but this option may carry a slightly higher fare.

Bus Operating Hours

Buses in Bratislava operate daily from early morning until late evening, with most buses running from around 4:30 AM until 11:30 PM. However, during weekends and public holidays, the schedule may differ slightly, and you may need to check the timetable for specific routes. For late-night travel, consider night buses (Lines N91–N99) that operate after regular hours.

Advantages of Traveling by Bus in Bratislava

1. Affordability: Bus fares are among the cheapest modes of public transport in Bratislava, especially if you buy day passes or group tickets.

2. Accessibility: With an extensive network of over 50 routes, buses offer easy access to many parts of the city, including areas not serviced by trams or the metro system.

3. Frequent Services: Buses run frequently throughout the day, with minimal wait times, making it a reliable and efficient mode of transport.

4. Wide Coverage: Buses can get you to both tourist attractions and local neighborhoods in Bratislava, from the airport to the Old Town, shopping malls, and residential districts.

Taxis

Getting Around Bratislava by Taxi: Comfortable and Convenient Travel

Taking a taxi in Bratislava offers a comfortable, convenient, and direct way to travel around the city, especially if you're carrying luggage or need to reach a location not well-served by public transport. While public transport in Bratislava is efficient and affordable, a taxi can be a great option when you're looking for privacy, speed, or door-to-door service.

Taxis in Bratislava: Overview and Availability

Taxis in Bratislava are readily available throughout the city, and they can be hailed on the street, ordered via phone, or booked through various taxi apps. The taxi fleet in the city is modern and well-maintained, offering a variety of vehicles, from standard cars to larger models for families or groups.

Some of the most popular taxi companies in Bratislava include:

- Hopin
- Taxi Bratislava
- Taxi 0905

In addition to regular taxis, ride-hailing services such as Bolt and Uber also operate in the city, providing more flexible and convenient options for getting around.

Taxi Terminals in Bratislava

Although taxis are not always stationed at specific taxi stands throughout the city like in some other cities, there are several designated taxi ranks near major locations, including transport hubs, shopping centers, and tourist spots. These taxi ranks are where you can find taxis waiting for passengers.

Key Taxi Terminals in Bratislava:

1. Bratislava Airport (M. R. Štefánik Airport):
    - Location: Taxis are available right outside the arrival hall at the airport.
    - Facilities: There are dedicated taxi stands outside the terminal, making it easy to hop into a taxi as soon as you arrive. Airport taxis are well-regulated, ensuring a safe and fair experience for travelers.
    - Booking: Taxis can also be pre-booked in advance via taxi companies or through ride-hailing apps like Bolt or Uber.
2. Main Train Station (Hlavná Stanica):
    - Location: The taxi rank is located just outside the main entrance of the Hlavná Stanica (Main Train Station).
    - Facilities: Taxis can be found in the designated area where passengers arriving by train can catch a cab directly to their destinations in the city.
3. Old Town (Staré Mesto):
    - Location: Although not a major taxi hub, taxis are often found near the central squares of the Old Town, such as Hlavné námestie (Main Square) or Františkánske námestie (Franciscan Square).
    - Booking: In busy tourist areas, you can often find taxis waiting near hotels, restaurants, and shopping districts.
4. Shopping Centers:
    - Location: Major shopping centers like Eurovea and Shopping Palace have taxi ranks outside the entrances. These areas are popular for both locals and tourists, so taxis are frequently available.
    - Convenience: These locations offer easy access to taxis for those shopping or dining in the area.

Taxi Costs and Fares in Bratislava

Taxi fares in Bratislava are relatively affordable compared to other European capitals. Fares are determined by a taximeter based on distance traveled, time taken, and any additional charges, such as waiting time or night-time rates.

Taxi Fare Breakdown:

1. Base Fare:
    - Cost: €1.50 – €2.00
    - The base fare starts when you get into the taxi, and this covers the first few kilometers of your trip.
2. Per Kilometer:
    - Cost: €0.90 – €1.20 per km
    - After the initial base fare, you'll pay a standard rate for each additional kilometer traveled.
3. Waiting Time:
    - Cost: €0.20 – €0.30 per minute
    - If the taxi has to wait for any reason (such as traffic or stops), you'll be charged based on how long the vehicle is stationary.
4. Airport Surcharge:
    - Cost: €1.00 – €2.00
    - Taxis from Bratislava Airport generally include a small surcharge for picking up passengers from the airport.
5. Night-time Surcharge:
    - Cost: Additional 10% – 20% on regular fares
    - If you're taking a taxi between 10:00 PM and 6:00 AM, expect a small increase in fare due to the night surcharge.
6. Example Fares:
    - From the Airport to the City Center: A taxi ride from M. R. Štefánik Airport to Old Town costs approximately €10 – €15, depending on traffic and route.
    - From Hlavná Stanica to Old Town: A taxi from the Main Train Station to the Old Town would typically cost around €5 – €7.
    - From Old Town to Bratislava Castle: A short trip from Old Town to Bratislava Castle would cost approximately €4 – €6.

Booking Taxis in Bratislava

While you can always hail a taxi on the street or at a taxi rank, it is often more convenient to pre-book a taxi, especially during peak times or if you're traveling from Bratislava's airport or train station.

1. Phone Bookings: You can call one of the city's reputable taxi services to arrange a pick-up at your location. Some of the popular taxi services in Bratislava include:

    - Taxi Bratislava: Phone: +421 903 300 300
    - Hopin: Phone: +421 905 300 300

2. Taxi Apps: You can also use ride-hailing services such as Bolt and Uber, which operate in Bratislava. These apps allow you to book a taxi directly from your phone and track your ride in real time.

Advantages of Taking a Taxi in Bratislava

1. Comfort and Convenience: Taxis offer a direct route to your destination, providing a level of comfort and privacy that public transport cannot match. This is particularly useful if you're traveling with luggage, during off-hours, or when you're in a hurry.

2. 24/7 Availability: Taxis are available at all times of the day and night, making them a reliable option, especially if you're traveling early in the morning or late at night.

3. Accessibility: With multiple taxi ranks across the city, you can easily find a taxi when you need one. Taxis are also great for reaching destinations not well-served by public transport, such as Bratislava's hilltops or outlying suburbs.

4. Safety: Licensed taxis in Bratislava are regulated, ensuring that the drivers are experienced and knowledgeable about the city. Ride-hailing services like Bolt and Uber provide an additional layer of security, as the apps offer driver information and ride tracking.

Bicycles

Getting Around Bratislava by Bicycle: Eco-Friendly and Scenic Exploration

Cycling in Bratislava offers an enjoyable, eco-friendly, and scenic way to explore the city. Whether you're an avid cyclist or just looking to enjoy a leisurely ride through its charming streets and green spaces, biking provides a unique perspective of Bratislava's historical and modern highlights. With bike lanes, cycling paths, and bike-sharing systems, getting around by bicycle in Bratislava is both practical and fun.

Bicycles in Bratislava: Overview and Routes

Bratislava has worked in recent years to improve its cycling infrastructure, with more bike lanes and cycle paths being developed across the city. Cycling is a popular activity for locals and tourists alike, with many visitors choosing to bike along the Danube River, through the Old Town, or to reach iconic spots like Bratislava Castle and Petržalka.

Bicycle routes are not only safe but also provide access to green spaces, making it easy for riders to move around while enjoying beautiful views of the city's parks and historic sites.

Popular Cycling Routes:

- Danube Cycle Path: This is one of the most scenic cycling routes, running along the Danube River, offering picturesque views of the riverbanks, castle, and the Old Town. It's also part of the larger EuroVelo 6, a European long-distance cycling route that runs from France to Romania.

- City Center Loop: A relaxing, flat ride that circles around the city center, passing through Bratislava's Old Town, parks, and key tourist spots. This route is perfect for those wanting a shorter, more leisurely ride.

- Petržalka to Old Town: This route connects the Petržalka district to the Old Town and the Bratislava Castle, allowing visitors to explore both modern and historic parts of the city while cycling through the scenic riverbanks.

Bike Rentals and Sharing Systems in Bratislava

For those who prefer not to bring their own bike, Bratislava offers a number of convenient bike rental and bike-sharing systems. These services are ideal for tourists who want to explore the city on two wheels without the hassle of transporting their own bike.

Bike-Sharing Systems:

- Rekola: Rekola is a popular bike-sharing service in Bratislava, providing red bikes scattered around the city. You can easily rent a bike via the Rekola app, which allows you to find available bikes, unlock them, and enjoy a ride.
    - Cost: Typically, €1 for the first 30 minutes, and €0.50 for each additional 30 minutes. There is also an option to buy a day pass for €6, which gives you unlimited rides for 24 hours.
- Citi Bike Bratislava: Another popular bike-sharing service is Citi Bike, which operates in the city, especially around major tourist attractions and transport hubs. You can rent a bike from one of the Citi Bike stations, which are located throughout the city.
    - Cost: €1 for the first 30 minutes, then €0.50 for each additional 30 minutes. A full-day pass for unlimited rides costs around €10.

Private Bike Rentals:

For those looking for a more personalized experience or higher-end bikes, there are bike rental shops in the city offering a range of bicycles, from city bikes to mountain bikes and electric bikes. These shops typically allow hourly, daily, or weekly rentals, with the option to return the bike at a different location within the city.

Some well-known bike rental shops in Bratislava include:

- Bratislava Bike Rentals
    - Cost: €10–€15 per day for a city bike.

- They offer delivery services to your hotel or desired location, which makes it more convenient for tourists.
- Cycling Bratislava
  - Cost: €12–€20 per day for a standard bike. Electric bikes are available for about €25 per day.

Bike Terminals and Parking in Bratislava

Bratislava has designated bike parking areas throughout the city, including bike racks and secured bike stations, making it easy to leave your bike safely while you visit shops, restaurants, or cultural sites.

Key Bike Terminals:

1. Old Town: Many parts of the Old Town have bike racks where you can park your bike while you explore historic sites such as Bratislava Castle, St. Martin's Cathedral, and the Old Market Hall.
2. Eurovea Shopping Center: Located near the Danube River, Eurovea provides bike racks for shoppers and cyclists alike. It's a convenient place to park your bike if you're heading to the mall or enjoying a riverside walk.
3. Bratislava's Public Transport Stations: Many tram and bus stations have bike racks or designated bike parking areas, allowing you to leave your bike safely while you hop on public transport for the next leg of your journey.

Bike Parking Costs:

- Most public bike racks are free to use. However, some bike-sharing services may charge a small deposit fee for renting a bike, which is refunded once the bike is returned to a designated station.

Chapter 5. Top Attractions

Bratislava Castle

Bratislava Castle: A Majestic Landmark Above the City

As Lukáš and Zuzana, two locals who have both grown up in the beautiful city of Bratislava, we can say without a doubt that Bratislava Castle is not just the city's most iconic monument but also a symbol of our rich history and heritage. Overlooking the Danube River and the Old Town, it has always been a place we enjoy visiting, whether it's for a peaceful walk, to marvel at the views, or simply to immerse ourselves in the castle's fascinating history.

Here's an overview of the castle, along with some of our personal insights, highlights, and practical information to help you make the most of your visit.

Overview of Bratislava Castle

Lukáš:
The Bratislava Castle stands majestically on a hill that offers panoramic views of the Danube River and the city below. This hill has seen thousands of years of history, dating back to the 9th century, making the castle a true historical treasure. The castle itself has undergone various reconstructions, particularly after the devastating fire in the 19th century. The current Baroque style of the castle is a result of these restorations, creating a stunning contrast with the older medieval structures.

For us locals, the castle is more than just a tourist attraction. It represents the heart of the city's history and culture. Bratislava Castle has played a key role in the past as a royal residence for Hungarian monarchs, a military stronghold, and even a governmental seat. Today, it houses the Slovak National Museum, with extensive exhibitions showcasing Slovak history, culture, and art.

Important Highlights of Bratislava Castle

Zuzana:
Visiting Bratislava Castle is an experience we cherish, not just because of its rich history, but also due to its unique highlights. Here are the key spots we think are essential for anyone visiting the castle:

1. The Castle Courtyard

Zuzana:
When you step inside the castle walls, you're greeted by the castle courtyard, which is beautifully designed with arches, fountains, and green spaces. It has an air of tranquility that allows you to take a moment to absorb the historical significance of the place. I love coming here in the early mornings when it's quieter, and you can really appreciate the peacefulness of the space.

2. The Museum and Exhibits

Lukáš:
As locals, we always recommend a visit to the Slovak National Museum located within the castle. The museum houses fascinating exhibits about Slovakia's history, art, and culture. The Historical Museum section is particularly interesting, showcasing medieval weapons, royal relics, and items from Slovakia's past as part of the Austro-Hungarian Empire. It's a great way to dive into the past and understand how Bratislava shaped the country's history.

Zuzana:
I enjoy the ethnographic and cultural exhibitions as well, which highlight Slovakia's folk traditions, art, and rural life. There are even some interactive displays, making it fun for both adults and children. If you're interested in Slovak heritage, the museum provides a great overview.

3. The Observation Deck and Views

Lukáš:
The castle's observation deck is definitely one of my favorite spots. From here, you can see a breathtaking panoramic view of Bratislava's Old Town, the winding Danube River, and even as far as Austria on a clear day. It's the perfect place to take photos, enjoy the sunset, or just relax and appreciate the beauty of the city.

Zuzana:
I can never get enough of the view from up there. It's truly one of the best views in Bratislava, with the river cutting through the city, the green hills in the distance, and the castle itself standing as a reminder of the past. Whether you're a local or a visitor, it's a sight that will take your breath away every time.

4. The Castle Interiors

Zuzana:
Inside the castle, the Royal Hall and Throne Room are stunning examples of Baroque architecture. These rooms offer a glimpse into the royal history of the castle, showing how it once served as a royal residence. The restored interiors are elegant, with chandeliers, paintings, and antique furniture. I especially love the Castle Chapel, which has a more intimate and spiritual feel to it.

Lukáš:
For me, the Royal Hall stands out. It's grand and awe-inspiring, giving you a sense of the castle's former glory as the seat of Hungarian kings. I enjoy taking my time here, imagining the history that unfolded within these walls.

How to Get to Bratislava Castle

Lukáš:
As locals, we usually walk to the castle from Bratislava's Old Town. It's a short, scenic walk that takes about 10 to 15 minutes depending on your pace. We love walking up Žižkova Street, which offers beautiful

views of the city as you approach the hilltop. The climb is gentle, and once you reach the top, the castle and the surrounding panoramic views make it all worth it.

Zuzana:
If we don't feel like walking, we take tram line no. 1, which stops near the castle. The Zámocká tram stop is just a few minutes away from the castle entrance, making it a quick and easy option for getting to the top.

For visitors unfamiliar with the area, the castle's location on the hill makes it easy to spot from different parts of the city. It's one of the tallest structures in the city, so it's hard to miss.

Costs and Admission Fees

Lukáš:
As locals, we often enjoy the castle grounds and the views for free. The castle's exterior and gardens are open to everyone without any charge, which is why it's a great place for a leisurely walk. However, if you want to visit the museum and explore the interiors, there is an entrance fee.

- Entrance to the Museum & Interior: €10 per adult
- Students, Seniors, and Groups: €5
- Observation Deck: €2 (The deck provides the most stunning views of Bratislava.)
- Family Ticket: €20 (This covers two adults and up to two children.)

Zuzana:
The museum and castle interior are definitely worth the €10 entry fee, especially if you're interested in learning about Slovakia's rich history. We both recommend purchasing a family ticket if you're traveling with children—it's great value for money.

Why We Love Bratislava Castle

Lukáš:
Bratislava Castle is one of those places that never gets old, no matter how many times you visit. For us, it's a symbol of the city's heritage and pride. Whether it's walking through the peaceful grounds, admiring the view, or diving deep into history, the castle offers something for everyone.

Zuzana:
I agree. It's not just a tourist attraction for us; it's an integral part of the city. Whenever we have friends or family visiting, we always take them to the castle because it represents everything we love about Bratislava—history, beauty, and a sense of place. It's a true gem in our city, and we're so lucky to have it as a backdrop to our daily lives.

St. Martin's Cathedral

St. Martin's Cathedral: A Key Symbol of Bratislava's History and Faith

As Lukáš and Zuzana, born and raised in the heart of Bratislava, we've always felt a deep connection to St. Martin's Cathedral. It's more than just a beautiful Gothic structure; it's a landmark that embodies the historical soul of our city. From its centuries-old significance to its architectural brilliance, we have visited this site numerous times, and each visit brings something new to admire. Here's a detailed look at why St. Martin's Cathedral holds such an important place in our hearts.

A Glimpse of St. Martin's Cathedral

Zuzana:
St. Martin's Cathedral, or Dóm sv. Martina, stands at the core of Bratislava's Old Town, a stunning reminder of the city's rich medieval heritage. The cathedral's origins date back to the 13th century, and its Gothic design makes it an architectural masterpiece. Its tall spire, which rises to a height of 85 meters, is an iconic feature of the Bratislava skyline. Whenever I walk through the Old Town, I feel a sense of pride as I look up at it, knowing this piece of history is right in the center of our city.

Lukáš:
Absolutely, Zuzana. As someone who grew up with this cathedral in the backdrop of daily life, it feels like the heart of Bratislava. Its Gothic arches and intricate stone carvings make it visually captivating, and the spires that reach for the sky serve as a reminder of Bratislava's past, especially its role as a key city in the Hungarian Kingdom. For me, the Coronation Hall is a particularly significant part of the cathedral, as it was here that many Hungarian kings were crowned during the 16th and 17th centuries.

Key Highlights of St. Martin's Cathedral

1. The Coronation Hall

Zuzana:
One of the most fascinating aspects of the cathedral is its Coronation Hall. Between 1563 and 1830, it served as the site of Hungarian royal coronations, making it a major historical landmark. Maria Theresa, one of the most important rulers in European history, was crowned here in 1741. Walking through this space gives me a sense of connection to centuries of history that shaped not only Bratislava but also Central Europe.

Lukáš:
The Coronation Hall really brings to life the historical significance of the cathedral. For me, it's one of the most memorable parts of visiting. I imagine the royal processions and the sense of anticipation in the air as kings and queens were crowned. It's remarkable to think that such important events took place here, in the same space that we now casually walk through.

2. The Stained-Glass Windows and Interior

Zuzana:
Inside, the cathedral's Gothic design continues to impress. The stained-glass windows, which date back to the 14th century, are an artistic masterpiece in themselves. They not only let light flood the interior but

also depict significant biblical scenes. As I sit inside, especially when the sun is shining through the windows, I feel like I'm surrounded by both art and history. It's one of the most peaceful places in Bratislava for me.

Lukáš:

I completely agree. I've always been fascinated by the details inside, especially the vaulted ceilings and altar. The atmosphere inside is always serene, whether you're there to appreciate the art or simply reflect. The Gothic arches create a sense of height and space that is awe-inspiring, and the quiet reverence of the place always seems to draw me in, even on busy days.

3. The Cathedral's Spire

Zuzana:

The spire of St. Martin's Cathedral is truly iconic. Rising 85 meters into the sky, it stands out against the skyline of Bratislava. The spire is covered in copper, which has developed a distinct greenish patina over time. From almost anywhere in the city, you can spot it. What's interesting is how it changes in appearance based on the time of day. Early morning light makes it glow, and during the golden hour at sunset, it becomes even more striking.

Lukáš:

For me, the spire is symbolic of how Bratislava's history has endured over the centuries. No matter how much the city changes, the cathedral's spire remains a steadfast point of reference for locals and visitors alike. On clear days, I enjoy walking along the Danube River with the spire in the distance, and it always serves as a reminder of Bratislava's medieval roots.

4. The Active Church Experience

Zuzana:

What I love about St. Martin's Cathedral is that it's not just a tourist attraction; it's still an active place of worship. The cathedral hosts regular masses, especially on Sundays, and it's where many locals go for religious services or special events like weddings and holidays. I often stop by for a moment of quiet reflection, and I find the atmosphere very calming. The cathedral still serves as a center of faith in the city.

Lukáš:

It's true. It's one of the few places in the city where I can feel completely immersed in the history and spirituality of Bratislava. There's something very powerful about seeing it function as a living, breathing place of worship, and the contrast between the medieval architecture and modern-day services is something special to experience.

How to Get to St. Martin's Cathedral

Lukáš:

The cathedral is located right in the heart of the Old Town, making it easily accessible by foot. From Hlavné námestie (the Main Square), it's only a 5-minute walk. You can also use the tram if you're coming from other parts of the city. The closest tram stop is Kapucínska, and from there, it's just a few minutes' walk to the cathedral. Alternatively, the Panská bus stop is also nearby.

Zuzana:
If you're visiting from the city center, you'll find that walking is the most pleasant way to get to the cathedral, as you'll be able to enjoy the historic streets and charming cafes along the way. For tourists, it's best to use the pedestrian zone, which brings you right to the doorstep of the cathedral. Public transportation is also an option, but walking through the Old Town gives you a more immersive experience.

Costs and Admission Fees

Zuzana:
For locals like us, the cathedral is free to visit, and we can walk in at any time, as long as there isn't a private event or service going on. There is no fee for general entry or for attending mass. However, there are some optional fees for those who want to explore the crypt or catacombs beneath the cathedral, which are an extension of the historical experience.

- General Entry: Free
- Catacombs/Crypt Access: €3
- Tram or Bus Ride: €0.90 (single ticket)

Why St. Martin's Cathedral Matters to Us

Lukáš:
St. Martin's Cathedral is not just a place to visit; it's part of what makes Bratislava feel like home. Whether it's the history it holds or the quiet moments it offers, it's a place we turn to time and time again. I find peace in its stillness, and I love how it bridges the past with the present, standing tall through centuries of change.

Zuzana:
For me, it's a symbol of Bratislava's identity. Walking past it or stepping inside always makes me feel grounded in the city's long history. It's incredible that something so ancient continues to play such a vital role in our lives today. We are lucky to live in a city where such a stunning piece of history is so easily accessible.

The Blue Church (Church of St. Elizabeth)

The Blue Church (Church of St. Elizabeth): A Masterpiece of Art Nouveau in Bratislava

As Lukáš and Zuzana, both born and raised in Bratislava, we can honestly say that The Blue Church (Church of St. Elizabeth) is one of our most cherished spots in the city. It's hard not to fall in love with this charming, pastel-colored gem that stands out amidst the more traditional architectural styles that dominate Bratislava. From its eye-catching exterior to its serene atmosphere inside, the Blue Church never fails to captivate. Whether we're passing by on foot or just stopping in for a moment of quiet reflection, this church holds a special place in our hearts.

Overview of The Blue Church

Zuzana:
The Blue Church, officially known as the Church of St. Elizabeth, is one of the most distinctive and beautiful landmarks in Bratislava. Completed in 1913, it was designed by the Hungarian architect Ödön Lechner in the Art Nouveau style, and it remains one of the most famous examples of this architectural movement in Slovakia. The church's standout feature is its stunning blue and white color scheme, which gives it a light, ethereal quality.

Unlike the more traditional churches you'll find in Bratislava, like the St. Martin's Cathedral, The Blue Church presents a softer, more whimsical face to the city. Its bright blue tiles and delicate white details create a refreshing contrast to the stone buildings around it. For us, living in this vibrant city, it's an architectural treasure that we can't help but appreciate each time we pass by it.

Lukáš:
It's hard to miss the church, and even if you've seen it a dozen times, it's always fascinating to look at again. The Art Nouveau style itself is quite rare for religious buildings in this part of the world, which is why the Blue Church stands out so much. The church has intricate mosaics and sculptures, all beautifully crafted to enhance its aesthetic appeal. For me, what truly sets it apart is the combination of its whimsical elegance and its deeply rooted historical significance. When you see the church, you don't just see a building – you feel like you're looking at a work of art.

Important Highlights of The Blue Church

1. The Art Nouveau Design and Blue Tiles

Zuzana:
The most striking feature of the Blue Church is undoubtedly its color. It's painted in a soft light blue with accents of white, giving it a fairy-tale-like appearance. The Zsolnay ceramics that cover the church's exterior were made by a famous Hungarian manufacturer and are used in artistic tile work across the entire church. The roof is especially noteworthy, with blue tiles arranged in a pattern that resembles fish scales. As a local, I've always admired how the church's exterior, with its whimsical style, seems to glow in the daylight, especially in the mornings when the light hits just right.

Lukáš:
The Art Nouveau style continues inside the church as well. It's not just about the exterior – the stained glass windows, the detailed frescoes, and the elegant sculptures all make the interior just as captivating. The way everything is so delicately designed gives it a very peaceful and intimate feeling inside. The light that pours in from the windows, combined with the soft pastel colors, creates an atmosphere that feels like you've stepped into a different world. As someone who grew up here, it's fascinating to me how such a unique building exists in a city that's home to much older, more traditional structures.

2. The Church's Spiritual and Historical Significance

Zuzana:
Although the Blue Church is smaller than some of the other churches in Bratislava, it still holds

significant historical and cultural value. It is still an active place of worship, regularly hosting mass services and special events, like weddings. There's a sense of calm reverence when you enter, and I think that's part of what makes this church stand out. People come not just for the architectural beauty, but also because it's a sacred space that offers a moment of peace in the midst of the bustling city.

Lukáš:

Yes, and I love the sense of history that's embedded in the church's walls. Even though it was built relatively recently in 1913, it still represents an important piece of Bratislava's religious history. The Church of St. Elizabeth is dedicated to St. Elizabeth of Hungary, and the rich Hungarian influence on the church's design is evident in many of its decorative details. I've attended a few weddings here, and there's a certain timelessness to the place – it feels like it connects the past to the present in a very meaningful way.

3. The Peaceful Atmosphere

Zuzana:

There's something magical about the atmosphere inside the Blue Church. It's quiet, almost like a sanctuary. Despite its popularity with tourists, the church has a way of feeling calm and private, allowing for a brief escape from the bustling city around it. I often come here for a moment of solitude, and it's a place that has always given me a sense of inner peace. For many locals, the church serves as both a place of worship and reflection, and it's one of the few places in the city where you can truly take a deep breath and feel centered.

Lukáš:

I agree. The church has a very peaceful vibe. Even when it's crowded outside, once you walk inside, there's a sense of quiet that makes it the perfect spot for introspection or just taking a pause from the busy streets. It's not a massive church, but it feels very welcoming and intimate, and I think that's part of its charm.

How to Get to The Blue Church

Zuzana:

The Blue Church is located in the eastern part of the Old Town, making it easy to reach from anywhere in the city. From Hlavné námestie (the main square), it's about a 10-minute walk. Simply head along Karadžičova Street, and you'll see it rising ahead. Its pastel blue exterior stands out among the surrounding buildings, so you can't miss it.

Lukáš:

If you prefer public transport, the closest tram stop is Karadžičova, which is just a 3-minute walk from the church. There are also several bus stops in the area, so getting there by bus is also quite convenient. However, we highly recommend walking if you're in the Old Town because you'll get to experience some of the quaint streets and cafés along the way, and it's a lovely walk!

Costs and Admission Fees

Zuzana:
Visiting the Blue Church is free of charge, which makes it even more inviting. As locals, we've visited many times without having to worry about any entrance fees. The church remains open to the public during most of the day, though access may be restricted during special events like weddings or services. If you are attending a mass, there's no charge to enter.

- General Entry: Free
- Special Events: Free, but sometimes limited access depending on the event

If you're using public transportation, a single tram or bus ticket costs about €0.90 for a 30-minute ride within the city center.

Why The Blue Church is Special to Us

Lukáš:
The Blue Church is a place that always leaves me feeling inspired, whether I'm simply admiring its exterior or stepping inside to take a quiet moment. It's such a unique architectural gem, and it's so refreshing to have a building like this in the middle of our city. Every time I pass by it, I'm reminded of Bratislava's rich cultural diversity and how the city continues to evolve while still preserving its roots.

Zuzana:
I feel the same way. The Blue Church is a special spot for us as locals. It's a place where history meets art, and it's one of those spots in Bratislava that feels like a true reflection of the city's charm. Whether you're coming here for a moment of peace or simply to admire its artistic beauty, it's an unforgettable experience. If you find yourself in Bratislava, this is definitely one of the must-see spots in the city.

Slovak National Gallery and Museum

Slovak National Gallery and Museum: A Deep Dive into Slovakia's Artistic Legacy

As Lukáš and Zuzana, both natives of Bratislava, we've had the privilege of experiencing the city's rich cultural offerings throughout our lives. One of the places that always stands out in our minds is the Slovak National Gallery (SNG). This museum, which houses an impressive collection of both Slovak and international art, is a true gem in our city. The building itself is a stunning example of modernist architecture, and the art within tells the story of Slovakia's evolving cultural and artistic history.

Overview of the Slovak National Gallery

Lukáš:
The Slovak National Gallery (SNG) is the largest and most prestigious art institution in Slovakia. Located in the heart of Bratislava, the gallery's collections span centuries of art history, showcasing everything from Medieval religious art to contemporary works. As a local, I've visited it countless times over the years, and I never get tired of it. The SNG is home to some of Slovakia's most famous artists, but also includes international works, making it an important cultural hub for the city. Whether you're a first-time

visitor or someone who's lived here for years, there's always something new and exciting to discover within its walls.

Zuzana:
Yes, and the building itself is as much a piece of art as the works it houses. The Slovak National Gallery occupies a beautifully restored section of the Old Town, with a modern structure that blends seamlessly with the historical surroundings. The SNG's collection is diverse, showcasing paintings, sculptures, graphic art, and applied arts. It's also home to some temporary exhibitions, which change regularly and offer fresh perspectives on both local and global art scenes. I've always loved how the gallery brings together Slovakia's cultural heritage and the world's artistic trends, creating a truly dynamic space. If you're a lover of art, this museum is not to be missed.

Important Highlights of the Slovak National Gallery

1. Rich Collection of Slovak Art

Zuzana:
One of the main reasons to visit the Slovak National Gallery is its extensive collection of Slovak artists. For me, the real highlight is seeing the works of Slovakia's own painters and sculptors. The medieval and baroque collections give a fascinating look into the country's religious art history, while the modern and contemporary pieces showcase the development of Slovak art in the 20th century. Artists like Ľudovít Fulla and Andy Warhol, who has Slovak roots, have their works represented here, which I find particularly interesting. You can witness how the evolution of Slovak identity is reflected in art, from the medieval period to the avant-garde movements of the 20th century.

Lukáš:
I also find the Slovak art collection especially enriching. The works of artists such as Martin Benka and Ján Koniarik really stand out to me. They depict Slovak landscapes, folk traditions, and historical moments that I'm personally connected to. Their art carries a sense of national pride and offers a deeper understanding of Slovakia's identity and history. It's more than just art; it's like looking through the country's history through a different lens. I also enjoy how the gallery's collection helps introduce international visitors to Slovak culture in a way that's both educational and entertaining.

2. Temporary Exhibitions

Zuzana:
Another fantastic thing about the Slovak National Gallery is its rotating temporary exhibitions. Every time I visit, there's usually something new to explore. These exhibitions often showcase international contemporary artists, as well as historical pieces that offer a fresh perspective on art movements. It's great for art enthusiasts who want to see a variety of art styles from across the world. For instance, they've hosted exhibitions dedicated to modern design, photography, and even experimental art forms. I find that these changing exhibitions add an element of surprise to each visit, keeping things exciting.

Lukáš:
I couldn't agree more. The temporary exhibitions are a big draw for me. For example, I've seen incredible pieces from artists like David Černý and Banksy. It's exciting to be able to experience such contemporary

art in a gallery that holds such a prestigious collection of traditional works. You get to see classic art alongside modern expressions, which makes each visit feel unique. It's an excellent way to stay up-to-date with current art trends and see how the global art scene intersects with local art movements.

3. The Museum's Location and Architecture

Lukáš:
The gallery itself is housed in a building that beautifully blends modern design with historical architecture. The Slovak National Gallery's headquarters are located in the Kollárovo námestie area, right next to the Old Town. It's an easy walk from the Main Square (Hlavné námestie), so if you're exploring Bratislava, it's very convenient to drop by. The architecture is striking—clean lines, minimalist design, and a blend of glass and concrete that complements the historical surroundings. The modern exterior really stands out, but it doesn't feel out of place; it's almost like it was meant to be part of this city's historical fabric.

Zuzana:
Yes, and the layout of the gallery is also thoughtfully designed. The museum's interior is spacious and inviting, allowing visitors to enjoy the art without feeling crowded. I particularly enjoy the airy open spaces and the light-filled galleries. The design of the building makes the art stand out even more, drawing attention to the works without distraction. As someone who spends a lot of time in the city, I appreciate how the Slovak National Gallery manages to blend modern art with the historical charm of Bratislava.

How to Get to the Slovak National Gallery

Lukáš:
Getting to the Slovak National Gallery is quite easy, especially if you're already in the Old Town. From Hlavné námestie (Main Square), it's just a 10-minute walk. If you're coming from the Bratislava Castle, it's about 20 minutes on foot. Simply head down Karadžičova Street, and you'll be right there.

If you prefer public transportation, the nearest tram stops are Karadžičova and Presbyterian Church, both of which are just a short walk from the gallery. You can also take a bus to Karadžičova.

Zuzana:
I recommend walking from the city center, as it's an easy stroll and you'll pass through some of Bratislava's charming streets along the way. The gallery's location in the city's cultural heart means you can easily make it a part of your walking tour around Bratislava's Old Town. It's very accessible, and if you're already exploring, it's an ideal stop for art lovers.

Costs and Admission Fees

Zuzana:
As locals, we enjoy visiting the Slovak National Gallery regularly because the entry fees are quite reasonable. Generally, the adult ticket price is around €6 for regular exhibitions, and €3 for concessions

(students, seniors, and children). However, there are special free days during the year, where entry is completely free, so be sure to check the gallery's website if you want to plan your visit around those days.

For temporary exhibitions, the price may vary slightly, usually ranging from €4 to €8 depending on the exhibition's scale and artists involved. It's worth it if you're interested in contemporary art or special collections.

Lukáš:
I agree, the cost of entry is definitely worth it, considering the quality of the exhibitions and the variety on offer. And for students, there are always discounts, which is great for those of us who want to visit more frequently without breaking the bank. It's one of those places where you get a lot of value for the price, and every time I visit, I leave with new insights or inspiration.

Why We Love the Slovak National Gallery

Zuzana:
The Slovak National Gallery is an absolute must-visit for anyone who's in Bratislava. Whether you're a local or a visitor, it offers a unique opportunity to explore both Slovak culture and global art movements. For us, it's not just a place to admire art, but a spot that helps us stay connected to the cultural pulse of our city. I'm proud of how the gallery showcases Slovakia's artistic talent while embracing international perspectives.

Lukáš:
It's one of the places in Bratislava that I always recommend to friends and tourists because there's so much to see, and every visit feels like an opportunity to discover something new. The Slovak National Gallery really captures the spirit of Bratislava: a city that honors its past while embracing the future. Whether you're an art lover or just looking to experience the cultural heart of the city, the gallery is the perfect spot to immerse yourself in Slovakia's artistic legacy.

The UFO Observation Deck

The UFO Observation Deck: A Unique Viewpoint in Bratislava

The UFO Observation Deck, perched atop the UFO Tower on the New Bridge (Most SNP) in Bratislava, offers one of the best vantage points to view the city. Standing 85 meters above the ground, it provides a stunning 360-degree panorama of Bratislava, the Danube River, and the surrounding landscapes, including the Carpathian Mountains. The tower, built in the early 1970s, is a significant symbol of the city's modern architecture, and it attracts both locals and tourists seeking breathtaking views, dining experiences, and historical context.

Important Highlights of the UFO Observation Deck

1. Stunning Panoramic Views

The UFO Observation Deck offers sweeping, 360-degree views of Bratislava and its surroundings. You can see the Old Town, Bratislava Castle, and the winding Danube River below. On a clear day, the Carpathian Mountains rise majestically in the distance, completing the stunning scene. The views make it one of the best places in the city to capture beautiful photographs and truly appreciate the geographical and architectural beauty of the area.

Zuzana:
One of the most incredible things about visiting the UFO Observation Deck is just how much you can see from up there. It's especially amazing at sunset when the golden light hits the Danube River and the cityscape lights up. It's the perfect spot to take it all in—whether you're admiring the historical Old Town or the modern urban areas like Eurovea.

2. Iconic UFO Design

The UFO Tower itself is an architectural masterpiece. Its saucer-like shape stands in stark contrast to the surrounding buildings, making it one of the most recognizable landmarks in Bratislava. Designed as part of the New Bridge, it symbolizes the modern, progressive era of the 1970s. Visitors often remark how striking and futuristic the structure appears, especially when seen from the Danube River or from within the Old Town.

Lukáš:
The tower's saucer design is something that's always fascinated me. It's a unique and bold shape that really stands out against the city's skyline. I think it's amazing that it was built during the Communist era, and today, it's one of the iconic structures in the city. I always enjoy watching tourists' reactions when they first see it – they can't believe how different it looks compared to anything else in Bratislava.

3. The UFO Restaurant

If you're looking to enhance your experience, the UFO Restaurant located just beneath the observation deck is the perfect place to enjoy a meal with a view. The restaurant serves a variety of European and Slovak dishes, allowing you to sample the local cuisine while soaking in the incredible vistas. Dining here is an experience in itself, as the views make it a memorable location for special occasions or a relaxing evening.

Zuzana:
I always recommend the UFO Restaurant to visitors. It's not only about the food – although I have to say, the Slovak specialties are great – but the experience of dining while overlooking the entire city. You can't beat that view. It's perfect for a romantic dinner or even a fun night out with friends.

4. The Bridge and Connection to the City

The UFO Tower is situated on the New Bridge, which is an essential crossing point over the Danube River, connecting Petržalka to the rest of Bratislava. The bridge itself is an architectural marvel, and from the observation deck, you can get a great view of it as it stretches across the river. The bridge's modern design complements the UFO Tower, making this spot a blend of both historical and modern Bratislava.

Lukáš:
When you look at the New Bridge, you start to realize how important it is to the city. It's one of the main

traffic links, and when you stand on the observation deck, you can see how much of Bratislava it connects. The UFO Tower adds a touch of futurism to a bridge that has been around for decades, making it feel like the city's old and new elements are right in front of you.

How to Get to the UFO Observation Deck

Zuzana:
The UFO Observation Deck is easily accessible from many parts of Bratislava. If you're in Old Town, it's about a 15-20 minute walk to the New Bridge. The bridge and UFO Tower are both easy to spot, thanks to the tall UFO-like structure perched at the top. You can also take public transport to the Petržalka district or Most SNP (New Bridge) tram or bus stops, which are just a short walk from the entrance.

If you're driving, there's parking nearby at the Petržalka side of the bridge, so it's easy to find a spot. From there, you can walk across the New Bridge to reach the UFO Tower.

Lukáš:
I recommend walking to the UFO Tower if you're in the Old Town. The walk along the Danube River is lovely, especially if the weather is nice. You can enjoy the views of the river and the city skyline while getting closer to the UFO Tower. Once you arrive, you'll see the elevator that takes you straight to the observation deck. The process is very quick and efficient.

Costs and Admission Fees

Zuzana:
Visiting the UFO Observation Deck is an affordable way to experience the best views in Bratislava. The current prices are:

- Adult Ticket: €8
- Reduced Ticket (students, seniors): €5
- Family Ticket (2 adults + 1 child): €18

If you're planning to enjoy a meal at the UFO Restaurant, there are combined packages that include entry to the observation deck as well as a meal at the restaurant. Prices for these packages vary depending on the menu you select, but they are generally a good value for the experience they offer.

Lukáš:
For what you get, I'd say it's a reasonable price. The views alone are worth the cost, and if you're planning to eat at the UFO Restaurant, the combined ticket offers good value. It's one of those places in Bratislava where the experience and the setting make the price feel worth it.

Why We Love UFO Observation Deck

Zuzana:
For anyone visiting Bratislava, the UFO Observation Deck is a must-see. The views are absolutely

breathtaking, and it gives you a unique perspective on the city's history and modern growth. Whether you're coming for the views, a meal, or just to admire the futuristic tower, this spot is a great way to appreciate the city in its entirety. It's a wonderful place to share with friends, family, or that special someone.

Lukáš:
 Exactly. It's one of those spots where you can really take your time and just soak in the beauty of Bratislava from a height. Whether you're a local or a visitor, it never gets old. I always find that the UFO Observation Deck offers something new, whether it's the way the city looks at different times of day or just the feeling of being so high up with the whole city beneath you. If you're in Bratislava, this is a place you shouldn't miss.

Primate's Palace

Primate's Palace: A Glimpse into Bratislava's Elegant Past

The Primate's Palace, located in the heart of Bratislava, is one of the city's most remarkable historical buildings. Dating back to the 18th century, the palace was initially the residence of the archbishops of Esztergom. With its striking neo-classical architecture and opulent interiors, the palace has long been a symbol of Bratislava's aristocratic heritage. Today, it houses the City Hall and is known for its stunning Hall of Mirrors, a true gem of Baroque design.

The palace stands as an excellent example of Bratislava's rich cultural history, offering visitors an opportunity to step into the grandeur of past centuries while experiencing the charm of one of the city's most beautifully preserved buildings.

Important Highlights of Primate's Palace

1. Neo-Classical Architecture

The Primate's Palace is a striking example of neo-classical architecture. Its facade features symmetrical lines, classical columns, and ornate detailing, all of which reflect the elegance and refinement of the time. The building's exterior is a visual treat, with pale yellow tones and intricate stone carvings. It's a perfect representation of the lavishness the aristocracy sought during the 18th century.

Zuzana:
 The building itself is really a beauty. It looks majestic yet understated in comparison to some of the grander palaces across Europe, but the neo-classical architecture really stands out to me. When you walk up to the palace, you can feel how the design evokes a sense of elegance and calm, and you can see how the archbishops of the past lived in such refined surroundings.

2. The Hall of Mirrors

One of the main highlights of Primate's Palace is its Hall of Mirrors, a room that exudes luxury and sophistication. The Hall, used for formal receptions and ceremonies, is a splendid example of Baroque design. With gold leaf decorations, crystal chandeliers, and its gilded mirrors, this room captures the grandeur of the palace. The reflective surfaces and rich decor add a certain brilliance to the space, making it an unforgettable part of the visit.

Lukáš:
For me, the Hall of Mirrors is definitely the standout. It's so grand and ornate – you can't help but feel like you've stepped back in time. The mirrors reflect all the light, creating a shimmering effect, and with the gold leaf detailing, it looks so opulent. I think it really shows how important ceremonial gatherings were in the palace's heyday.

3. The Palace Gardens

Although the interior of Primate's Palace is remarkable, the gardens behind the palace are also a peaceful retreat. The small, beautifully maintained garden area offers visitors a break from the hustle and bustle of Bratislava's Old Town. With fountains, greenery, and lovely flowerbeds, the garden provides an oasis in the middle of the city, allowing guests to relax and enjoy the tranquility of the palace's surroundings.

Zuzana:
When I take visitors to the Primate's Palace, I always recommend spending some time in the gardens. They're not as grand as other palace gardens around the world, but they're beautiful in their simplicity. It's a quiet place, perfect for a little stroll after touring the inside of the palace.

4. City Hall and Public Access

Since the Primate's Palace serves as the home of the City Hall, it's also the site for various public events, such as art exhibitions, city receptions, and cultural events. The palace is more than just a historical site; it's an active part of Bratislava's public life. Visitors can often find art exhibitions or concerts hosted within its elegant halls, making it a cultural hub as well.

Lukáš:
It's also interesting that the Primate's Palace isn't just a historical building; it's still used for civic purposes today. It really brings a sense of living history to the city. I've attended a couple of art exhibitions there, and they always seem to perfectly complement the historical atmosphere of the palace itself.

How to Get to the Primate's Palace

Zuzana:
The Primate's Palace is located just a short walk from Bratislava's Old Town. If you're staying in the city center, you can easily reach it by walking down Bratislava's main pedestrian street, Hlavná Ulica, which leads directly to the palace. The palace is situated on the Old Town Square and is very close to other prominent landmarks like St. Michael's Gate and the Main Square. Public transportation options, including trams and buses, are also nearby, with stops at Hlavná Stanica (main train station) or Petržalka.

Lukáš:
I always recommend walking to the Primate's Palace from Old Town since it's a pleasant walk and you get to see all the lovely streets. It's also easy to combine a visit to the palace with a tour of the Old Town

because it's so close to everything. There are no buses or trams needed if you're already in the heart of the city.

Cost and Admission Fees

Zuzana:
The Primate's Palace is relatively affordable to visit. The typical admission fees are:

- Adult Ticket: €5
- Reduced Ticket (students, seniors): €3
- Children under 6: Free

There may also be additional charges for special exhibitions or guided tours. It's recommended to check in advance if you're planning to attend any events or exhibitions being held at the palace.

Lukáš:
The price to visit the Primate's Palace is very reasonable for what you get. I think it's a good deal, especially since you get to enjoy both the historic building and the public exhibitions that are often on display. For just €5, it's definitely worth taking the time to explore the palace's beautiful rooms and gardens.

Why We Love Primate's Palace

Zuzana:
The Primate's Palace is one of my favorite spots in Bratislava because it's such a beautiful, serene place that connects visitors with the city's rich history. From the elegant architecture to the magnificent Hall of Mirrors, it's a must-see when in Bratislava. It's also in the perfect location, right in the middle of Old Town, so you can easily explore the area before or after your visit.

Lukáš:
I completely agree. It's such a wonderful place to learn about the city's history while also soaking in the Baroque beauty of the building. And like Zuzana said, it's a relaxing spot amidst all the hustle and bustle of the Old Town, which is what makes it so special. If you're ever in Bratislava, the Primate's Palace should definitely be on your list of places to visit.

Devin Castle and the Danube River Views

Devin Castle and the Danube River Views: A Historic Gem Overlooking the Danube

Devin Castle is one of the most iconic and historically significant landmarks in Bratislava. Situated at the confluence of the Danube River and the Morava River, this majestic castle has stood for centuries, offering sweeping views of the surrounding landscapes. The castle ruins date back to the 9th century, and the site played an important role in both Slovak and European history. Over the years, Devin has witnessed dramatic moments in history, including Roman occupation, medieval battles, and modern restoration efforts.

The location itself, perched on a cliff overlooking the rivers, offers visitors an extraordinary view of the surrounding forests and hills, making it a popular destination for tourists and locals alike. Today, Devin Castle is a museum, showcasing various exhibits related to the region's history, archaeology, and the castle's development through the ages.

Important Highlights of Devin Castle

1. Breathtaking Views of the Danube River

One of the most captivating aspects of Devin Castle is the panoramic view of the Danube River. From the castle's towers, visitors can enjoy an unobstructed view of the Danube, the Morava River, and the border area between Slovakia and Austria. The sight of the rivers winding through the landscape, with the forest-covered hills and the Austrian countryside in the distance, is breathtaking. The view from the castle serves as a reminder of the castle's strategic importance in controlling river routes.

Zuzana:
Every time I visit Devin Castle, I am struck by the views. The Danube winds through the valley so peacefully, and the Morava River meets it in such a beautiful, natural way. If you take your time, you can sit on the castle walls and watch the water flow for hours. It's a peaceful place to just reflect on the history of the area.

2. Castle Ruins and the Tower

Though much of Devin Castle is in ruins, the parts that remain offer a glimpse into the castle's former grandeur. The most notable part is the watchtower, which rises above the ruins, allowing visitors to climb to the top for even better views of the rivers and surrounding nature. The castle's walls and bastions provide insight into the architecture of medieval fortresses, while the strategic location shows why this castle was important for military defense in the past.

Lukáš:
I love the feeling of standing in the watchtower and looking out over the landscape. When you're up there, you get a sense of why the castle was so important in its time. The views make you feel connected to the past, as you imagine how the guards would have watched for invaders from that exact spot.

3. Museum Exhibits

Inside Devin Castle, there are exhibits that detail the history of the site, including its role in the Roman Empire and its significance as a border fortress during the Middle Ages. The museum also covers the Archaeological Finds from the area, with ancient tools, ceramics, and even Roman ruins discovered nearby. You can learn about the castle's various phases of construction, from its Roman fortifications to its more recent reconstructions.

Zuzana:
The museum is a great way to learn more about the history of Devin Castle and the surrounding region. There's always something new to discover, and it's amazing to see how this place has evolved over the centuries. You'll find information about everything from the Roman period to its modern restoration.

4. The Roman Well

A particularly interesting feature at Devin Castle is the Roman Well, located within the castle grounds. This well dates back to the time when the castle was part of the Roman Empire's defense system. The well, still functional today, provides a fascinating historical connection to the Roman occupation of the region and gives visitors a chance to connect with the ancient past of the site.

Lukáš:
I think the Roman Well is one of the most fascinating parts of the castle. It's incredible to think that something so old is still in use today. Standing there, you can almost imagine the Romans drawing water from it centuries ago. It's a special part of the castle that adds to its historical significance.

How to Get to Devin Castle

Zuzana:
Devin Castle is located about 10 kilometers from Bratislava city center, making it an easy trip for anyone staying in the city. You can get there by bus, which runs from Bratislava and takes about 20 minutes to reach the castle. The bus stop for Devin Castle is located near the Devin village entrance, and from there, it's just a short walk to the castle itself.

If you prefer to drive, it's easy to get to Devin by car, and there is parking available near the castle. Alternatively, there are cycling routes that follow the Danube River, and some visitors enjoy cycling along the river to get to the castle, making it a great option for nature lovers.

Lukáš:
If you're in Old Town, I'd recommend the bus because it's quick and simple. I personally enjoy cycling to Devin Castle along the Danube River—it's an easy, scenic ride, and it gives you the chance to enjoy the river views on the way there. Either way, the trip is short and gives you time to take in the beautiful surroundings.

Cost and Admission Fees

Zuzana:
The cost to visit Devin Castle is quite affordable. As of now, the ticket prices are:

- Adult Ticket: €10
- Reduced Ticket (students, seniors): €5
- Family Ticket (2 adults + 1 child): €20

There is also an additional fee for guided tours or special exhibitions, though these fees are generally quite reasonable. It's a good idea to check for discounts or special events that may be happening when you plan your visit.

Lukáš:

It's a great value for such a historic site. The ticket price is low compared to some other castles around Europe, and you get access to both the ruins and the museum. If you take a guided tour, you'll learn even more about the castle's history, which is totally worth the extra cost.

Why We Love Devin Castle and the Danube River Views

Zuzana:

I can't recommend Devin Castle enough. The views of the Danube River and Morava River alone make it worth the visit, but there's so much history packed into the castle as well. Whether you're looking to enjoy the panoramic vistas, explore the museum, or simply stroll through the castle grounds, it's a spot that captures the essence of Bratislava's rich history and natural beauty. It's a peaceful escape from the city's hustle and bustle.

Lukáš:

Exactly. Devin Castle is such an iconic part of Bratislava's heritage. The combination of stunning views, ancient ruins, and history makes it a perfect day trip. It's one of those places where you can really immerse yourself in the past while also enjoying the surrounding beauty. Whether you're a local or a tourist, it's always a great experience.

Chapter 6. Exploring Bratislava's Neighborhoods

The Old Town: Charm and History

The Old Town: Charm and History

Bratislava's Old Town is the heart and soul of the city, a place where history and charm meet in a delightful blend of cobblestone streets, medieval buildings, and centuries-old landmarks. Walking through the Old Town is like stepping into another era, where every corner reveals something fascinating. As a local, I never tire of this part of the city — whether I'm taking a casual stroll along Slovenská ulica, sipping coffee at a sidewalk café, or exploring the many historical sites that make Bratislava's Old Town so special.

One of the first things that strikes you about the Old Town is its charming atmosphere. The streets are lined with colorful buildings that span several centuries of architectural styles, from medieval and Baroque to Renaissance and Gothic. The narrow alleys and cobblestone streets give the neighborhood a timeless feel, with each building offering a glimpse into the city's rich past. You'll often come across small boutique's, art galleries, and quaint cafés nestled in the heart of this historical setting, making it a wonderful place to wander and explore at your own pace.

One of the most iconic landmarks in the Old Town is the Bratislava Castle, which stands proudly atop a hill overlooking the city. The castle dates back to the 9th century and has played a central role in Slovak history. While the castle itself is a must-see, the views from the hill are equally spectacular, offering a panoramic perspective of the Danube River, Old Town, and the distant Carpathian Mountains. The Castle Gardens, located at the base of the castle, are also a peaceful place to relax, enjoy the greenery, and take in the beauty of the city.

Another historical gem in the Old Town is St. Michael's Gate, the last remaining medieval city gate, which offers a glimpse into the city's past defenses. This gate dates back to the 14th century and is one of the most photographed spots in Bratislava. Right next to it is the St. Michael's Tower, which houses a small museum where you can learn more about the history of the gate and the city's medieval fortifications.

For lovers of religious history, St. Martin's Cathedral is another must-visit landmark in the Old Town. This stunning Gothic cathedral, with its beautiful stained-glass windows and intricate architecture, has witnessed many important moments in Slovak history, including the coronation of Hungarian kings. The cathedral's tower offers some of the best views of the city, and the nearby square, Hlavné námestie, is a lovely spot to enjoy a leisurely coffee while soaking in the atmosphere.

If you're a fan of art and culture, The Old Town has an array of museums and galleries to explore. The Slovak National Museum, for instance, provides fascinating insights into the country's history and culture, while the City Museum gives visitors an in-depth look at Bratislava's past, from its Roman origins to its modern-day transformation.

A visit to the Old Town would also be incomplete without a trip to Hlavné námestie, the main square. This lively pedestrian-only square is the heart of the Old Town, surrounded by beautiful buildings, shops, and cafes. It's often filled with local vendors and hosts various events and festivals throughout the year. The square is also home to the Old Town Hall, an impressive Renaissance building that now houses the City Museum.

How to Get to the Old Town

The Old Town is easily accessible from almost anywhere in Bratislava, and it's well-connected by public transport. If you're coming from the city center, the Old Town is just a short walk away. The most convenient way to reach it is by tram, with several routes, such as lines 1, 4, and 8, running through the area. The bus lines 32, 39, and 93 also serve the Old Town area, so getting there by public transport is quick and easy.

For those staying near the train station, it's a 15-minute walk to the Old Town. The walk takes you through Karadžičova Street and across the Most SNP (New Bridge), offering picturesque views of the Danube River along the way.

If you're coming by car, the Old Town is easily accessible via Karadžičova Street, and there are several paid parking options available in and around the area. However, keep in mind that traffic can be a bit congested, especially during the peak tourist season, so taking public transport or walking is often the most convenient option.

Petržalka: Modern City Vibes

Petržalka: Modern City Vibes

Petržalka, located on the southern bank of the Danube River, is one of Bratislava's most dynamic and rapidly evolving neighborhoods. Over the years, this area has transformed from a primarily residential district with utilitarian high-rise buildings to a vibrant urban hub full of modern amenities, green spaces, and cultural spots. Often overshadowed by the Old Town's historic charm, Petržalka offers a fresh, modern energy that makes it a unique part of the city to explore.

One of the highlights of Petržalka is its urban architecture, marked by the large panelák buildings from the Communist era. These imposing apartment blocks give the area a somewhat industrial, utilitarian feel, but over time, new developments and revitalized spaces have infused it with a fresh, modern character. While the area's urban aesthetic might not have the picturesque beauty of the Old Town, its distinct city vibe holds a unique appeal.

Eurovea, a large shopping mall and entertainment complex, is a prime feature of the neighborhood. Located on the banks of the Danube River, this modern development offers an upscale shopping experience with international and local brands, trendy cafes, and a selection of restaurants. The mall is also home to a cinema and a riverfront promenade where you can walk and enjoy stunning views of the river and the Bratislava skyline. It's a perfect spot for both locals and visitors looking to unwind in a modern, vibrant space.

Another key feature of Petržalka is Sad Janka Kráľa Park, one of the oldest public parks in Slovakia. Despite its history, the park has been updated with modern amenities, providing a great escape for nature lovers. With wide walking paths, peaceful spots to relax, and lush greenery, it's a favorite destination for families, joggers, and anyone looking to take a break from the hustle and bustle of city life.

The neighborhood also boasts a growing cultural scene. Local galleries, independent theaters, and creative spaces contribute to Petržalka's modern identity. Places like the Petržalka Cultural Center host performances, exhibitions, and workshops, celebrating the area's increasingly vibrant artistic community. The development of contemporary art spaces here offers a refreshing contrast to the more traditional, classical art in the Old Town.

Petržalka's riverside area provides a relaxing spot for both locals and tourists to stroll, cycle, or simply enjoy the fresh air. The Danube promenade, located near Eurovea, offers panoramic views of the river, perfect for a peaceful walk. In the evenings, the promenade becomes a popular place for relaxation, with cafes lining the waterfront offering a perfect setting to enjoy a coffee or a drink as the sun sets.

How to Get to Petržalka

Petržalka is easily accessible from the city center of Bratislava. If you're already in the Old Town, it's just a 10 to 15-minute tram or bus ride to reach the heart of Petržalka. Popular tram and bus lines that connect the city center with Petržalka include the tram lines 2, 4, and 8, and buses like 52 and 91. You can catch these trams and buses from Most SNP, Central Station, or Hodžovo námestie in the city center.

Alternatively, if you prefer cycling, Petržalka is easily reachable by bike, thanks to the dedicated bike lanes that run along the Danube River. The cycle path provides a scenic route and is ideal for anyone who wants to experience the area from a different perspective.

For those arriving by car, Petržalka can be accessed via Karadžičova Street or the D2 highway. If you're driving, you'll find parking facilities around major spots like Eurovea Mall, making it convenient for those visiting by car.

If you're coming from Bratislava's main train station, it's a quick 10-minute taxi ride or 20-minute walk to the district. Alternatively, Petržalka Train Station offers direct access to the neighborhood from various regional and international destinations, making it a perfect entry point for those arriving by train.

Nové Mesto: Bratislava's Growing District

Nové Mesto: Bratislava's Growing District

Nové Mesto, or "New Town," is one of Bratislava's most dynamic and rapidly developing districts, offering a fascinating contrast to the historic charm of the Old Town. This area is where the modern side of the city truly comes to life, with a mix of contemporary buildings, business districts, and cultural spots. Over the years, Nové Mesto has evolved from a primarily residential neighborhood into a thriving urban hub, making it an exciting part of Bratislava to explore.

As I walk through Nové Mesto, I can't help but feel the energy of the area. It's a district that showcases the modern face of the city—with sleek office buildings, shopping malls, and wide streets designed to handle the hustle and bustle of daily life. But at the same time, it retains a sense of community and green spaces, offering a balance between urbanization and nature. From a local's perspective, the district is still growing, with new residential areas and commercial developments popping up regularly.

One of the key highlights of Nové Mesto is Polus City Center, one of the city's largest shopping malls. Located right in the heart of the district, it offers a wide variety of retail shops, restaurants, and entertainment options, including a cinema. It's a go-to place for locals who want to enjoy a modern shopping experience or have a quick bite. As a resident of Bratislava, I often pop into Polus to pick up something, catch a movie, or simply enjoy the lively atmosphere.

Another feature of Nové Mesto that I appreciate is its green spaces. While the district is known for its urban development, it also offers parks and recreational areas that provide a breath of fresh air in the middle of city life. Kramáre Hill, for example, is a quiet retreat offering some of the best panoramic views of Bratislava, including the Old Town and Danube River. It's an excellent spot for a morning jog or just to unwind after a busy day.

For those interested in sports, Nové Mesto has a few excellent options, including Tehelné Pole, the home stadium of Slovan Bratislava, one of the city's top football teams. This modern stadium is not only a place for sports fans to catch a game but also hosts concerts and other major events, adding to the district's vibrant energy.

In terms of culture, Nové Mesto is also home to several museums and art galleries, though it's not as saturated with historical landmarks as the Old Town. The Slovak National Gallery, located near the edge of Nové Mesto, is one of the major cultural institutions in the area, showcasing a wide range of Slovak and international art. It's a great place to visit if you want to dive deeper into the artistic scene of Bratislava.

How to Get to Nové Mesto

Getting to Nové Mesto from the city center is straightforward and convenient. Public transport is the easiest way to reach the district, with several tram and bus lines connecting it to other parts of Bratislava. If you're coming from Hlavné námestie (Main Square) or the Old Town, a tram ride is a great option. Tram line 4 runs directly through the district and takes you right into the heart of Nové Mesto. The tram ride is typically around 10–15 minutes, depending on where you start your journey.

Alternatively, there are a number of bus routes that connect Nové Mesto to other neighborhoods in Bratislava. Buses such as lines 32 and 93 will get you to Polus City Center and other spots in the district in no time.

If you prefer to cycle, Nové Mesto is an excellent area for it. There are dedicated bike lanes along major streets like Karadžičova and Vajnorská, making it easy to navigate the district while enjoying the ride. It's a great option for anyone looking to explore the area at a more leisurely pace.

For those arriving by car, Nové Mesto is accessible via Vajnorská Street or Karadžičova Street, which connect directly to the city center and other major districts. There are public parking lots and parking garages throughout the district, especially near Polus City Center and Tehelné Pole, making it convenient for those visiting by car.

Lastly, if you're coming from Bratislava's main train station (Hlavná stanica), it's a quick 15–20 minute tram ride or a 10-minute taxi ride to reach Nové Mesto.

Ružinov: Parks, Lakes, and Local Life

Ružinov: Parks, Lakes, and Local Life

Ružinov, a district in eastern Bratislava, is a peaceful yet vibrant area that offers a refreshing blend of urban life, nature, and local charm. Often regarded as one of the city's most pleasant residential neighborhoods, Ružinov combines modern conveniences with lush green spaces, making it a perfect spot for both locals and visitors looking to escape the bustle of the city center while still enjoying the city's offerings.

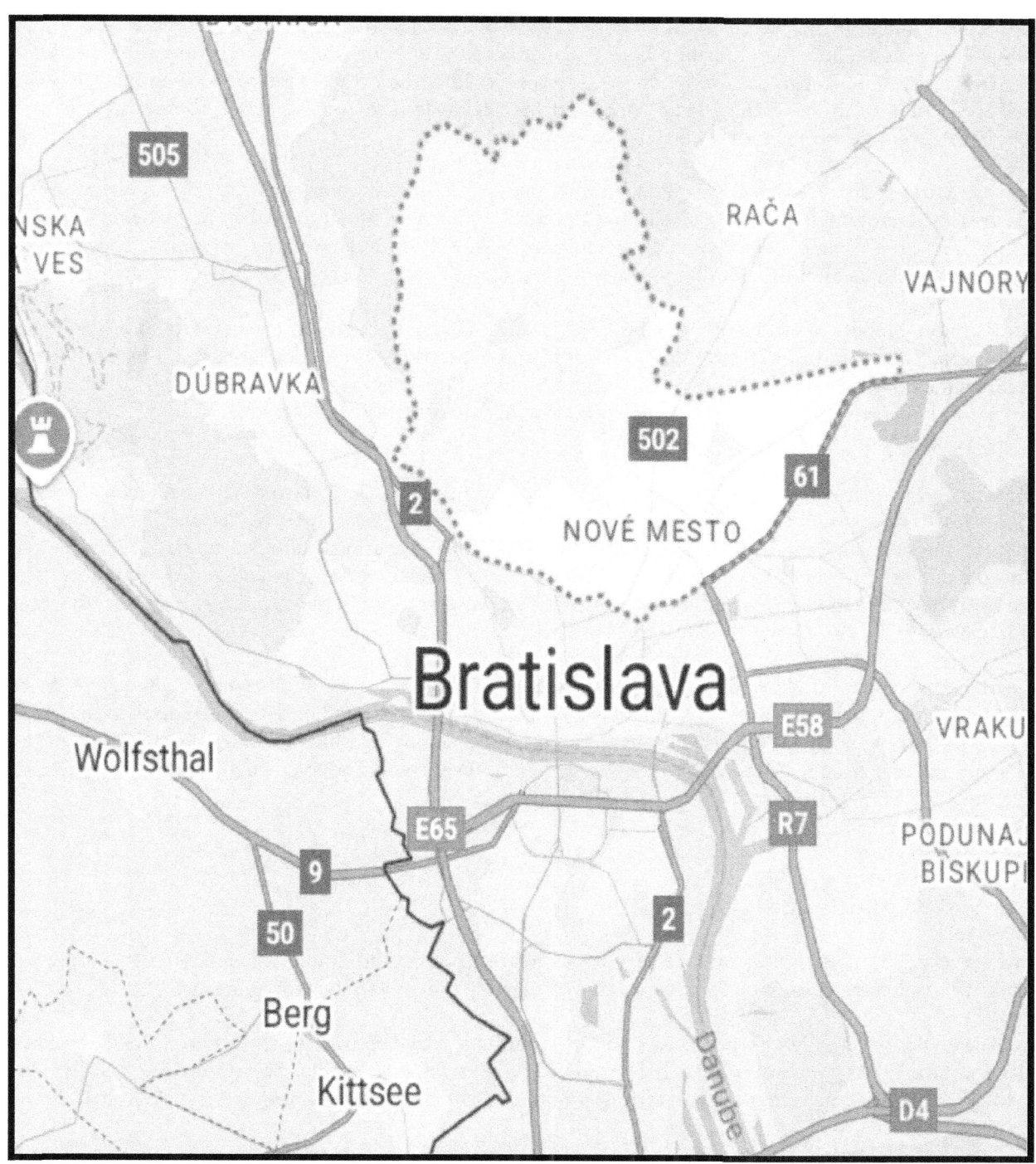

The area is best known for its abundance of parks, lakes, and recreational areas, which make it one of the most family-friendly districts in Bratislava. As a local, I appreciate how easy it is to unwind here, surrounded by nature, and how much the neighborhood has to offer in terms of community and convenience.

A key feature of Ružinov is Štrkovec Lake, one of the largest lakes in Bratislava. This peaceful, man-made lake is surrounded by a spacious park, making it an ideal spot for a leisurely walk or a relaxed day by the water. People come here for a morning jog, to bike around the lake, or simply to sit by the water and enjoy the tranquility. On a warm day, you'll often see locals walking their dogs, families with children playing, and even couples enjoying the scenic surroundings. Štrkovec Lake is also home to several cafés and restaurants where you can enjoy a meal with a view of the water.

Nearby, Ružinov also has Lake Kuchajda, another popular spot for outdoor activities. Much like Štrkovec, this lake is surrounded by green space that's perfect for picnics, leisurely walks, or just unwinding in nature. The area around Lake Kuchajda is equipped with playgrounds, walking paths, and sports fields, making it a go-to location for families and anyone looking to relax or be active in a peaceful environment.

One of the highlights of Ružinov is the Janko Kráľ Park, a charming green space that features wide open areas perfect for recreational activities. It's not just about nature—the park also has a number of sports facilities such as tennis courts and football pitches, as well as cycling paths, making it ideal for anyone looking to stay active. There are also benches and shaded areas where you can relax after a workout, enjoy a good book, or simply enjoy the green surroundings.

Apart from its green spaces, Ružinov has a local, community-oriented vibe that makes it feel welcoming. It's far less touristy than the city center, yet it offers a rich array of local cafés, restaurants, and shops that cater to the everyday needs of its residents. Trhovisko Ružinov, a bustling local market, is the perfect example of this. It's where locals gather to shop for fresh produce, flowers, baked goods, and more. This market reflects the area's focus on community life and is a great spot to pick up some fresh ingredients or simply observe the day-to-day life of Bratislava's residents.

For those who love modern amenities, Ružinov is also home to several shopping centers like Avion Shopping Park, one of the largest in Bratislava, offering a variety of retail outlets, supermarkets, cinemas, and more. It's a convenient place for locals to run errands, shop for clothing, or catch a movie. It's not just a shopping hub, though—Avion also hosts occasional events and activities that bring the community together.

How to Get to Ružinov

Ružinov is easily accessible from the city center of Bratislava. The public transport network makes it simple to reach, with several bus and tram lines connecting the area to the rest of the city.

From the Old Town, you can reach Ružinov by tram lines 4 and 8, which pass through the district and take you directly to popular spots such as Štrkovec Lake or Lake Kuchajda. The tram ride typically takes 15 to 20 minutes depending on the starting point. You can catch these trams at Most SNP or Hodžovo námestie.

Alternatively, if you prefer buses, several routes also serve the area. Bus lines 50, 52, and 93 are some of the most commonly used routes to get to Ružinov. These buses make stops throughout the district, offering easy access to places like Avion Shopping Park and Janko Kráľ Park.

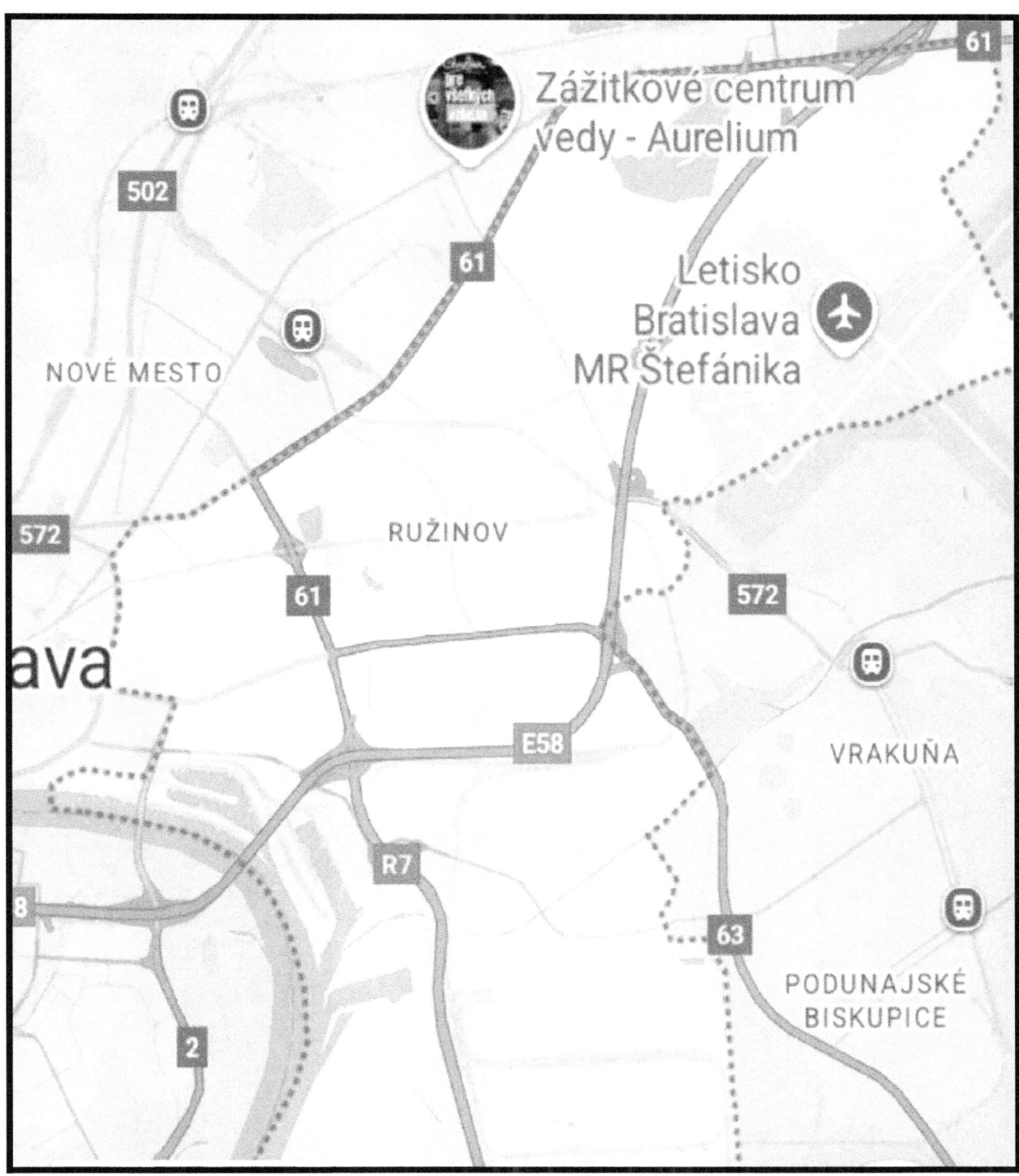

Cycling is also a great way to explore Ružinov, thanks to its dedicated bike lanes along major streets like Vajnorská and Prievozská. The Danube Bike Trail runs nearby, so you can easily connect to other parts of the city by bicycle. Whether you're cycling around Lake Kuchajda or cruising through local parks, it's a relaxing way to enjoy the district's natural beauty.

For those traveling by car, Ružinov is easily reached via the D1 highway or Vajnorská Street, both of which connect to the district from the city center. There are plenty of public parking facilities available near major shopping centers like Avion, as well as around the lakes and parks, so getting around by car is simple.

Chapter 7. Culture and Entertainment

Slovak Traditions and Folklore

Slovak Traditions and Folklore

Slovakia is a country steeped in rich traditions and folklore that tell the story of its history, culture, and the people who have lived here for centuries. The Slovaks, with their deep connection to the land and rural way of life, have cultivated a treasure trove of customs, crafts, music, dances, and beliefs that reflect their values, their respect for nature, and their love for celebration. These traditions, many of which continue to be practiced today, offer a window into the heart of Slovakia's identity.

Traditional Clothing (Kroj)

One of the most iconic aspects of Slovak folklore is its traditional clothing, known as kroj. These outfits, often seen at festivals or folk events, are richly embroidered and vary across different regions of Slovakia. The embroidery is usually symbolic, with patterns that represent the region's customs, culture, and the natural world. For example, motifs of flowers, animals, and stars can often be seen.

The women's kroj is typically a colorful dress made from cotton or linen, paired with petticoats, headscarves, and aprons. The men's kroj, on the other hand, includes a white shirt, trousers, a vest, and a hat. The garments are often accented with beaded jewelry or metal clasps that enhance their beauty. Kroje are more than just clothes; they are a visual representation of Slovakia's agricultural roots and its connection to community and family traditions.

Folk Music and Instruments

Slovak folk music has been an essential part of the nation's culture for centuries. The melodies are deeply tied to the country's rural life, often narrating stories about the beauty of nature, the challenges of hard work, love, and family. One of the most well-known elements of Slovak folk music is the fujara, a unique, long wooden flute that produces deep, resonating sounds. This instrument, associated with shepherds in the mountainous regions of Slovakia, is so significant that it was even listed as a UNESCO cultural heritage.

In addition to the fujara, other traditional instruments like the cymbalom (a type of hammered dulcimer), violin, and accordion are commonly used in Slovak folk bands. These instruments create the lively, toe-tapping tunes that are a hallmark of Slovak dance music. Folk songs are typically choral, with group singing being a significant part of gatherings, especially during festivals or social events. The lyrics often express the joys and sorrows of everyday life, making the music incredibly emotional and relatable.

Folk Dances

Slovak folk dances are as rich and varied as the country's music. Dances like the polka, horehron, and dukelské are traditional forms that are still regularly performed at festivals, weddings, and community events. These dances are lively, energetic, and full of intricate footwork. They often tell stories of courtship, nature, and rural customs. The dances are performed in pairs or groups, with participants wearing the kroj and accompanying the music with lively movements.

One of the most popular dance festivals is the Východné Folklore Festival, where dancers from all over Slovakia come together to showcase their regional folk dances. The dances often involve rapid foot stamping, spinning, and jumping, all performed in rhythm with traditional music. The passion and joy with which these dances are performed reflect the Slovak love for life and community.

Traditional Crafts

Slovakia has a long tradition of handmade crafts, many of which are still practiced today. Woodworking, pottery, embroidery, and weaving are common crafts that have been passed down through generations. In particular, the wooden carvings from the Central Slovakia region are highly regarded. The designs are often intricate and are inspired by nature, such as animals, flowers, and religious symbols.

Pottery, particularly from Cierna nad Tisou, is known for its distinctive red and black clay creations. The pieces range from simple mugs to decorative sculptures, often featuring geometric patterns and earthy tones. Meanwhile, Slovak embroidery is known for its vibrant and detailed designs. The technique is particularly significant for the Zemplín region and is used to decorate tablecloths, bed linen, and traditional garments. This craft symbolizes the importance of family, as many of these handmade items are passed down from one generation to the next.

Folk Festivals and Celebrations

The Slovaks love to celebrate their traditions, and this is evident in their many folk festivals throughout the year. One of the most famous is the Shrovetide Carnival (Fašiangy), which is held before Lent and is full of lively parades, masks, music, and dancing. It's a time for the community to come together and celebrate life before the solemn period of fasting.

Another key festival is Easter, which is marked by unique traditions such as the Easter Monday whipping. On this day, men and boys gently whip women and girls with willow branches, a custom believed to promote fertility and health. The whipping is followed by a celebration with food, drinks, and often painted Easter eggs, which are a beautiful form of Slovak folk art. These decorated eggs, known as kraslice, are created using various techniques, including wax-resist and wooden carving, and are displayed as a symbol of renewal and spring.

Superstitions and Beliefs

Like many cultures, Slovak folklore is rich in myths and superstitions. People believed that spirits and nature's forces had a direct impact on their lives, and many customs were designed to protect against evil spirits. For instance, it was common to place amulets or protective charms on homes, farms, or barns to ward off negative energy.

Some traditions involve rituals tied to the changing of the seasons, such as the burning of the effigy during the spring festival, symbolizing the death of winter and the rebirth of life. People would often make straw dolls, representing winter, and burn them in symbolic acts to ensure a good harvest and a prosperous year.

Festivals and Events: What's Happening in Bratislava

Bratislava Music Festival

Bratislava Music Festival: A Local Perspective

The Bratislava Music Festival is one of the most anticipated events in Slovakia, drawing music lovers from around the world to the capital every autumn. Held annually in September and October, this festival is a celebration of classical music, featuring an impressive line-up of orchestras, soloists, and composers. From world-renowned musicians to inspiring young artists, the festival brings top-tier performances to the heart of Bratislava. To give you a closer look at this cultural gem, we've gathered three locals' perspectives on what the festival has to offer.

From Peter, a Classical Music Enthusiast

"I've been attending the Bratislava Music Festival for years, and it never fails to impress. Held in late September, it marks the start of autumn, and the cool weather makes it the perfect time to enjoy indoor performances. Every year, the festival attracts top orchestras from around the world—last year, we had the honor of listening to the Vienna Symphony Orchestra perform. The acoustics in the Reduta Concert Hall are superb, and there's something magical about listening to a symphony in such a historic venue."

"The festival offers a variety of performances, from large orchestral pieces to chamber music and even opera. I always look forward to the concertos with famous soloists, such as violin or piano performances. Last year, I attended a recital by a renowned pianist, and it was so intimate that you could hear every note clearly. It's an experience that connects you to the music in a way that feels personal and profound."

"For classical music lovers like me, the festival is a highlight of the year. The performers are of the highest caliber, and the atmosphere at each concert is filled with excitement and appreciation. Whether you're a seasoned music aficionado or just someone who enjoys live music, the Bratislava Music Festival offers something for everyone. The quality and variety of performances make it an unmissable event."

From Jana, a Young Professional

"Even though I'm not a classical music expert, I love how the festival has something for everyone. When I first attended a few years ago, I was surprised by how accessible and welcoming the whole experience felt. The atmosphere in Bratislava during the festival is lively, with both locals and visitors from abroad coming together to enjoy the arts. I often meet up with friends before or after the concerts to talk about what we've heard, and it's a great way to connect with others."

"The festival is held in a variety of venues around the city, including the Slovak National Theatre and even outdoor stages in the Old Town. I love how the events take place in both grand concert halls and smaller, more intimate settings. The performances are top-notch, and it's amazing to see so many international artists come to Bratislava. Last year, I attended an open-air concert in Hodžovo námestie, and it was such a fun experience. The setting, the music, and the crowd all came together in a way that made it feel like part of the city's culture."

"One thing I really enjoy about the festival is that there's more than just the big-ticket concerts. There are free outdoor performances, and I've seen some incredible smaller performances by talented local musicians. These events make the festival feel inclusive, and it's a great way to experience music without spending a lot of money."

From Marek, a Long-Time Resident

"Having lived in Bratislava my whole life, I can tell you that the Bratislava Music Festival has become an essential part of the city's cultural calendar. It's always held at the start of autumn, and there's something about the cool air and golden leaves that make the festival feel even more special. When the festival comes to town, the city feels alive with music—it's not just about the concerts but also the whole cultural atmosphere that it creates."

"The festival offers such a wide range of performances. I've attended everything from symphonies and operas to smaller, more intimate chamber music performances. One of my favorite things is seeing how the festival evolves each year. There's always a mix of traditional and contemporary music. One year, I attended a concert featuring modern composers alongside Beethoven's classics, which was an exciting contrast. It's amazing to see how the festival blends the old with the new, creating a dynamic experience."

"For me, the festival is also a celebration of Bratislava's musical heritage. The Slovak Philharmonic Orchestra is one of the main performers, and I'm always proud to see them shine on the international stage. The orchestra's performances are something special, and it feels like a moment of pride for our city. Also, the festival gives Slovak musicians a chance to showcase their talent, and I always look forward to seeing the young local performers who are starting to gain international recognition."

What the Festival Offers

- World-Class Performances

The festival attracts top-tier orchestras, soloists, and ensembles from around the world, bringing the best of classical music to Bratislava. You can hear symphonies from prestigious orchestras, including the Vienna Symphony Orchestra and the London Philharmonic Orchestra, as well as performances by renowned conductors and soloists.

- Variety of Venues

The festival takes place in a variety of settings, from the historic Reduta Concert Hall and the Slovak National Theatre to smaller, more intimate venues in the Old Town. This gives you the opportunity to experience the music in different atmospheres, each offering a unique charm.

- Opera and Ballet

The festival showcases outstanding operatic and ballet performances, with both classic and contemporary works being presented at the Slovak National Theatre. It's a wonderful opportunity to enjoy top-tier productions in a beautiful setting.

- Chamber Music and Recitals

If you prefer smaller, more personal performances, the festival offers intimate chamber music concerts and solo recitals. These performances allow you to enjoy intricate pieces up close in intimate venues, where the sound feels more personal.

- Outdoor Concerts and Free Events

One of the highlights of the festival is its accessibility. Many performances take place outdoors, and there are free concerts scattered around the city, making the music available to a broader audience. It's a great way to enjoy live performances in the open air, especially in Bratislava's charming Old Town.

- Educational Programs

The festival also focuses on education, offering masterclasses and workshops for young musicians. It's an excellent opportunity for up-and-coming artists to learn from established masters, making the festival not just a celebration of music but also an important educational platform.

The Bratislava Music Festival offers something for everyone: whether you're a classical music aficionado like Peter, a young professional like Jana looking for a mix of culture and fun, or a longtime resident like Marek who enjoys seeing the city come alive with music. Each year, the festival continues to showcase the rich cultural landscape of Bratislava and provides visitors with an unforgettable musical experience.

Folk Art Festival (Východné Folklore Festival)

Folk Art Festival (Východné Folklore Festival): A Local Perspective

The Východné Folklore Festival, also known as the Folk Art Festival, is one of the most exciting and colorful events in Slovakia. Held every year in Východné, a village in the eastern part of the country, this festival celebrates Slovakia's rich cultural heritage through folk music, dance, crafts, and local traditions. The festival brings together performers, artisans, and visitors from all over Slovakia and beyond.

Typically held in early summer, in June, the festival offers an unforgettable experience for anyone interested in Slovakia's folklore traditions. Let's hear from three locals on what this vibrant festival has to offer.

From Ľubica, a Traditional Folk Dance Enthusiast

"I look forward to the Východné Folklore Festival every year—it's the heart and soul of our local traditions. Held at the start of summer, in June, the weather is always perfect for spending time outdoors. The festival is held in the village of Východné, and for three days, the whole place is buzzing with music, dance, and colorful costumes. The air is full of the sound of fiddles, accordions, and the rhythm of traditional folk dances."

"The highlight for me is always the performances by local folk dance groups. These dances tell stories of our past, of life in the villages, and of our ancestors' customs. The costumes are beautifully made, often embroidered with intricate patterns that reflect the history of the region. It's amazing to see the younger generations take part in these dances, passing down these traditions to keep them alive."

"But it's not just about watching the dances. The festival gives people the chance to learn and even join in. There are folk dance workshops, where anyone—no matter their experience—can try their hand at the steps. For me, it's always a great opportunity to reconnect with my roots and share the joy of our culture with others."

From Martin, a Local Craftsman

"I've been a part of the Východné Folklore Festival for many years, and I can't say enough about how special this event is. It's not just about music and dance—it's a celebration of everything that makes Slovak culture unique. As a craftsman, I participate in the festival by showcasing my hand-made wooden items, which include everything from carved figurines to traditional utensils. There's something so fulfilling about seeing people appreciate the craftsmanship and the stories behind the items."

"The festival is also a fantastic place to experience traditional Slovak crafts. Alongside the music and dance, there are artisan stalls set up by local craftspeople, where you can see how people have been creating art and practical items by hand for generations. I'm always amazed by the variety of crafts on display—whether it's pottery, embroidery, or woven textiles, it's an amazing opportunity to see these skills in action and learn about their importance to our culture."

"What makes the festival even more special is the way it brings together the younger generation with the older one. Many of the younger artisans who grew up learning these crafts are now sharing their skills and knowledge, making the festival feel like a living, breathing tradition."

From Katarína, a Music Teacher and Local Resident

"As a resident of Východné, the Folk Art Festival is something I look forward to every year—it's a time when our village becomes a true showcase of Slovak culture. The festival takes place in June, and it's an incredible mix of folk music, local traditions, and community spirit. What's especially lovely is that it's not just for tourists; it's something the whole village gets involved in. You see everyone, from children to grandparents, getting involved in some way, whether by performing or supporting the event."

"For me, the best part of the festival is the traditional folk music performances. The sounds of cimbal (a type of hammered dulcimer), fiddles, and flutes fill the air, and there's something so moving about hearing these instruments play the folk tunes that have been passed down through generations. There are also choral performances from local choirs, which give the festival a sense of nostalgia, reminding me of my childhood."

"One of the things I love most about the festival is the way it connects the past and present. You'll find traditional folk bands playing alongside younger, more modern groups that blend folk with contemporary styles. It's a wonderful reminder that these traditions are still evolving and living on in new and exciting ways."

What the Východné Folk Art Festival Has to Offer

- Traditional Folk Music and Dance Performances. The heart of the Východné Folk Art Festival lies in its folk music and dance performances. Visitors can enjoy performances from local folk dance groups, as well as traditional folk musicians playing instruments like the cimbal, fiddle, accordion, and flute. The dancers wear vibrant, traditional costumes, each region of Slovakia having its own unique style. The performances are both energetic and meaningful, as each dance tells a story from Slovakia's past.
- Folk Dance Workshops. One of the most enjoyable aspects of the festival is the opportunity for visitors to get involved in the tradition of folk dancing. There are workshops where you can learn some of the basic steps, making it a fun and interactive experience. People of all ages can join in and feel the joy of dancing to live music with the locals.
- Traditional Crafts and Artisans. For those interested in Slovakia's handicrafts, the festival features artisan stalls where you can find a wide range of handmade goods, from wooden sculptures and carvings to woven textiles and embroidery. Many of the artisans demonstrate their craft, giving you a deeper appreciation of the techniques and traditions that have been passed down through generations.
- Food and Local Delicacies. No festival is complete without good food, and the Východné Folklore Festival is no exception. Local food vendors offer traditional Slovak dishes like bryndzové halušky (potato dumplings with sheep cheese), pirohy (dumplings stuffed with various fillings), and kapustnica (sauerkraut soup). It's the perfect way to fuel up before heading back to the dance floor or checking out more artisan stalls.
- Choral and Vocal Performances. Another key feature of the festival is the choral performances. Local choirs perform traditional folk songs that highlight Slovakia's rich vocal heritage. The harmonies and melodies bring a sense of unity and nostalgia to the festival, as many of these songs have been passed down for generations.

- Family-Friendly Atmosphere, The festival is a celebration for all ages. Children can enjoy the folk dances, crafts, and music, while the entire family can learn about Slovakia's cultural heritage through interactive exhibits and performances.

Bratislava International Film Festival

Bratislava International Film Festival: A Local's Perspective

The Bratislava International Film Festival (BIFF) is one of the most prominent cultural events in the city, attracting cinephiles, filmmakers, and artists from around the world. Held annually, the festival showcases a diverse selection of films, ranging from high-profile international productions to independent and experimental works. Whether you are a local or a visitor, this festival provides a unique opportunity to immerse yourself in the world of cinema. Let's dive into what this festival offers through the perspectives of three locals, who each bring their own experiences and insights into the event.

From Peter, a Film Buff

"The Bratislava International Film Festival is my favorite time of year in the city. Held every November, it's a great way to close the year, and the crisp autumn air only adds to the atmosphere of the event. What I love about BIFF is that it's not just about big blockbusters—it's about films that you won't typically see in mainstream theaters. It's a place where independent filmmakers get a chance to shine, and there's always a sense of discovery. I've seen films here that I would never have imagined watching otherwise, and they've stayed with me long after the credits rolled."

"The festival's programming is diverse. It features documentaries, short films, and feature-length movies from around the world. Every year, I look forward to the competition sections where the best new films from directors all over the world compete. You get the chance to see emerging talent before their films hit the international stage, and it's exciting to be part of that discovery. Plus, there are special screenings of cult classics, and sometimes even retro films that are restored and shown in stunning new formats. It feels like a celebration of cinema in all its forms."

"I also enjoy the panels and masterclasses that are often held alongside the screenings. They allow you to engage with filmmakers, actors, and critics who are often very open about the creative process. It's a fantastic opportunity to learn about the behind-the-scenes work that goes into making a film, and I always leave those sessions feeling more knowledgeable and inspired about the art of filmmaking."

From Jana, a Young Professional

"The Bratislava International Film Festival is such a fun and lively event. It's held in November, which I think is perfect timing—everything's cooler, the city's quieter, and the festival gives it a buzz of excitement. What I love about BIFF is how inclusive and accessible it is. Even though the films are international, the festival doesn't feel like something for just film enthusiasts. There's always something for everyone, from experimental cinema to family-friendly movies. I've attended screenings with friends who aren't particularly into films, and we all end up having a great time."

"One of my favorite parts is the film screenings in unique venues. While there are traditional theaters like the Kino Lumière and Kino Mladosť, there are also screenings in more unusual locations, like art galleries or open-air venues during warmer days. It creates a very different experience from a regular cinema trip, and it's refreshing to watch films in such settings. Plus, I love how the festival brings people together—it's not uncommon to meet filmmakers, actors, and fellow movie lovers from all over. It's always a fantastic chance to network and chat with people who share your love of cinema."

"Another thing that makes the festival stand out is the program of short films. These are often experimental or avant-garde pieces that push the boundaries of storytelling. It's not something I would usually seek out, but the festival's diversity makes it easy to explore different genres and styles of film that I wouldn't normally watch. It's a great way to broaden your horizons as a film lover."

From Marek, a Long-Time Resident

"Having lived in Bratislava for so long, I've seen the Bratislava International Film Festival grow and evolve into one of the city's most important cultural events. It takes place every November, and it feels like the city really comes alive with it. You'll see more people on the streets, film posters in cafes, and everyone talking about which screenings they're going to. The buzz is contagious, and it feels like the whole city is participating in the celebration of film."

"What I appreciate most is the wide variety of films that are shown. BIFF isn't just focused on one genre or type of filmmaking—it spans everything from experimental shorts to dramatic feature films to international documentaries. Last year, I went to a screening of a Slovak documentary about the country's history during the 20th century, and it was fascinating to see the local perspective on such important events. You wouldn't usually expect to see that kind of film in a mainstream cinema, so BIFF really provides a chance to watch something special and thought-provoking."

"I also appreciate how the festival helps highlight Slovak filmmakers. It's always inspiring to see our local talent getting recognition on an international stage, and BIFF is a platform that really supports them. There are always screenings of Slovak films, and some even go on to win awards. As a local, it fills me with pride to see our filmmakers gaining exposure and recognition on the global scene."

What the Bratislava International Film Festival Has to Offer

- International Films and Premieres: The festival showcases an eclectic selection of films from all over the world, offering audiences a chance to watch international premieres and some of the best films from top festivals like Cannes, Venice, and Berlin. Whether it's cutting-edge independent films, award-winning documentaries, or feature films from both established directors and emerging talents, BIFF offers something for every film lover.
- Diverse Programming: One of the most appealing aspects of BIFF is its varied program. The festival offers screenings in multiple categories, including competition films, documentaries,

short films, and experimental cinema. Whether you enjoy gripping drama, poignant documentaries, or abstract experimental films, you'll find something that resonates with you at BIFF.
- Film Screenings in Unique Locations: The festival is known for its unique screening locations, which range from traditional movie theaters like Kino Lumière and Kino Mladosť to more unconventional spaces such as art galleries and open-air cinemas. These settings enhance the cinematic experience and provide a more immersive and intimate viewing environment for festivalgoers.
- Workshops and Panels: BIFF goes beyond just film screenings—it also offers panels, workshops, and masterclasses for aspiring filmmakers and industry professionals. These events are a great way to learn from filmmakers, actors, and producers about the craft of filmmaking and the global film industry. It's also an excellent opportunity to hear behind-the-scenes stories and get insider knowledge.
- Slovak Film Focus: While the festival brings films from across the world, it also highlights Slovak cinema. With a dedicated section for Slovak films, BIFF gives local filmmakers a chance to present their work on an international platform. It's a wonderful opportunity for Slovak filmmakers to showcase their talent and gain recognition, and for locals to support and celebrate their homegrown cinema.
- Awards and Recognition: The festival's award ceremonies are always a big draw. The top films in various categories receive accolades, and some of these films go on to international fame and success. It's exciting to be a part of the festival as the winners are announced, and it feels like you're part of a special moment in the film world.
- Networking and Community: For those in the film industry, BIFF offers ample opportunities for networking. Filmmakers, actors, critics, and film lovers all converge in Bratislava to enjoy the festival, creating an environment ripe for creative exchanges. It's not just about watching films; it's about joining a community that shares a passion for cinema.

Pohoda Festival

Pohoda Festival: A Local's Perspective

The Pohoda Festival is Slovakia's largest and most popular music festival, held annually in Trenčín, a historic city in the western part of Slovakia. It takes place every July, just as the summer reaches its peak, offering the perfect mix of warm weather and a vibrant atmosphere. Pohoda has grown into a celebrated cultural event, attracting tens of thousands of music lovers, artists, and people of all backgrounds. From its diverse lineup of music genres to its focus on sustainability and cultural exchange, Pohoda is much more than just a music festival—it's a full celebration of art, community, and creativity. Here's a look at Pohoda through the perspectives of three locals who attend the festival year after year.

From Peter, a Long-Time Music Enthusiast

"For me, Pohoda is the highlight of the summer. Held every year in early July, it's the best time to be outdoors in Slovakia, and there's something truly magical about the vibe at this festival. What I love about Pohoda is its diverse music lineup. Whether it's rock, electronic, hip-hop, or even world music, the festival has something for every type of music lover. I remember one year I was blown away by The Chemical

Brothers, and the next, I was dancing to Sigrid—the variety of acts is amazing. You can spend the whole weekend jumping from one stage to another and discover something new every day."

"Pohoda isn't just for mainstream music either. Every year, they showcase indie bands, up-and-coming artists, and even local Slovak performers. It's great to see Slovak musicians getting the chance to perform next to international headliners. I especially love the smaller stages where you can watch an unknown artist and feel like you've discovered a new favorite. The festival's emphasis on diversity, from the music to the people, really sets it apart from other festivals in Europe."

"Another thing that stands out to me is the atmosphere. Despite being one of the largest festivals in Slovakia, Pohoda never feels overcrowded or chaotic. It's always a very relaxed and friendly environment. People come to enjoy the music, the art, and the culture, but it's never about the size or the crowds—it's about creating a memorable experience. You see groups of friends, families, and solo travelers all coming together, and it's just an incredible mix of people who share a love for music and creativity."

From Jana, a Creative Professional

"As a creative person, what makes Pohoda special for me is how much it embraces art and creativity. While the music is obviously the main attraction, there's so much more to see and do at the festival. Every year, there are stunning art installations scattered throughout the festival grounds. You can wander through the venue and find interactive sculptures, street performances, and theater productions that give the festival a unique, almost magical atmosphere. One year, I got completely lost in an art installation about light and shadow, and it felt like I was in another world."

"Pohoda is also a hub for workshops and cultural exchange. I've attended a few workshops that touch on different topics like eco-fashion, sustainability, and artistic expression. These workshops are an amazing way to meet like-minded people and learn new things in a fun, informal setting. I think the festival does a wonderful job of merging art, music, and social issues. There's always a focus on environmental and cultural sustainability, and it's inspiring to see how they encourage people to think about these important topics while enjoying the festival. The talks and panel discussions are always so thought-provoking."

"The festival also promotes diversity and inclusivity, which I think is one of the reasons it has such a strong following. You see people from all walks of life, whether it's different generations, cultures, or backgrounds, coming together to celebrate art and music. That sense of belonging and shared experience is something I truly appreciate about Pohoda."

From Marek, a Local Resident of Trenčín

"Living in Trenčín for most of my life, I've watched Pohoda grow into one of the most important events in Slovakia. The festival has really become part of the city's fabric, and every summer, the entire town gets excited for it. As a local, I can say that there's this special energy in the air leading up to the event. People from all over the country and abroad come to Trenčín, and the town itself feels like it's full of life and creativity."

"Pohoda is so much more than just a music festival; it's a celebration of Slovak culture alongside international art. For instance, the festival gives Slovak artists a platform to showcase their work, which I think is great for local culture. Last year, I was proud to see a number of Slovak bands playing alongside major international acts. It's exciting to see how the festival brings global music and Slovak traditions together in one place."

"I also love the festival's environmental efforts. Pohoda has made a conscious effort to reduce its carbon footprint, whether it's through solar-powered stages, waste reduction programs, or encouraging people to bring reusable water bottles. As someone who cares about the environment, I think it's great that Pohoda is using its platform to raise awareness about sustainability in such a fun and engaging way."

"Another personal favorite for me is the food at Pohoda. As a local, I really appreciate the variety of Slovak dishes on offer, from bryndzové halušky (potato dumplings with sheep cheese) to kapustnica (traditional cabbage soup). There's also international food, and you'll find plenty of vegetarian and vegan options. It's one of the best places to sample Slovak cuisine while enjoying live music."

What the Pohoda Festival Has to Offer

- Diverse Music Lineup:

Pohoda is known for its incredible range of musical genres. Whether you're into indie rock, electronic, hip-hop, or Slovak folk music, you'll find something to enjoy. The festival brings together global superstars and emerging local talents, and with multiple stages set up across the grounds, you can experience a wide variety of performances all day long. There's something for everyone, whether you're a casual listener or a serious music enthusiast.

- Art Installations and Cultural Events

One of the standout features of Pohoda is its artistic and cultural programming. The festival grounds are filled with art installations, street performances, and even live theater. Every year, new creative projects and installations pop up, making it a festival that engages both the eyes and the mind. If you're someone who loves to explore new forms of art and creativity, Pohoda offers a whole world to discover beyond the music.

- Workshops and Talks

Pohoda is not just about music—it's also a platform for learning and discussion. The festival hosts a variety of workshops, panel discussions, and talks on topics ranging from sustainability to social issues. For example, you might find workshops on eco-friendly fashion, cooking classes, or discussions about the impact of climate change. It's a great opportunity to learn something new while engaging with creative minds from around the world.

- Sustainability Focus

The festival takes environmental issues seriously. Pohoda is known for its efforts to reduce its carbon footprint, such as using solar energy for some of its stages, offering recycling stations throughout the venue, and encouraging zero waste practices. It's a festival that values sustainability and encourages its attendees to think about their impact on the planet while enjoying the event

- Family-Friendly Atmosphere

While the festival attracts people of all ages, it's particularly family-friendly. Pohoda offers activities for children, including interactive performances, creative workshops, and a variety of family-friendly music. It's a great place for families to spend time together, surrounded by music, art, and a welcoming atmosphere.

- Slovak Cuisine and International Food

The festival grounds are full of food stands offering a wide variety of dishes, from traditional Slovak meals like bryndzové halušky and goulash, to international street food. Vegetarian, vegan, and gluten-free options are also available, making it easy for everyone to find something they can enjoy while spending the day at the festival.

The Arts: Galleries and Theaters, and Music Venues

Galleries:

Bratislava City Gallery: A Local's Perspective

The Bratislava City Gallery (Galéria mesta Bratislavy) is one of the most prominent cultural spaces in the city, showcasing a diverse range of Slovak and international art. Located in the historic center of Bratislava, the gallery occupies several buildings, each offering a unique perspective on contemporary and classical art. It hosts a variety of exhibitions, ranging from modern art to classical Slovak works, and regularly features temporary shows, art events, and workshops.

Highlights:

- The gallery is housed in several locations, including the Palace of the City Gallery and the Mirbach Palace, both rich in history and architecture.
- It showcases works by Slovak painters, sculptors, and photographers, often including major names such as Ľudovít Fulla, Jozef Czáky, and Martin Benka.
- Temporary exhibitions are regularly held, offering a fresh look at contemporary art trends.
- The gallery also offers a pleasant café where you can relax after exploring the exhibits.

How to Get There:

The Bratislava City Gallery is easily accessible from the city center, just a short walk from the Main Square (Hlavné námestie). You can reach it by:

- Walking: The gallery is located within walking distance from most central locations in Bratislava.

- Trams: You can take tram lines 4, 5, or 1, and get off at Zochova station, which is a 5-minute walk to the gallery.

Cost (as of 2025):

- General Admission: €5
- Concessions (students, seniors, children): €2.50
- Free Entry: On the first Wednesday of every month, entry is free.

From Hana, a Local Art Enthusiast:

"I visit the Bratislava City Gallery regularly. It's a fantastic spot for art lovers. I enjoy walking through the Mirbach Palace and admiring the works of classic Slovak artists. The atmosphere is so peaceful, and I often stop by their café afterward to unwind. It's also very affordable compared to other European galleries!"

From Peter, a Long-Time Resident:

"I love that the gallery isn't just about art—it's also about the architecture of the buildings it's housed in. The Palace is a hidden gem, and whenever I bring visitors, they're always amazed by how beautiful the interior is. The exhibitions are top-notch, and the fact that there's free entry once a month is a huge bonus!"

Slovak National Gallery: A Local's Perspective

The Slovak National Gallery (Slovenská národná galéria) is one of the most important cultural institutions in Slovakia, showcasing Slovak art from the Middle Ages to contemporary works. Situated in the heart of Bratislava, the gallery offers a comprehensive collection of paintings, sculptures, and photography by both Slovak and international artists. With its mix of permanent and temporary exhibitions, it's a must-visit for anyone interested in the rich art history of Slovakia.

Highlights:

- Permanent Exhibitions feature Slovak art from various periods, including the medieval, Baroque, Romantic, and Modernist eras.
- The gallery also houses temporary exhibits showcasing contemporary art, photography, and multimedia pieces.
- One of the most notable features is the unique architecture of the building, blending historical design with modern elements.
- The gallery hosts regular art events, workshops, and educational programs for children and adults alike.

How to Get There:

The Slovak National Gallery is located in the city center of Bratislava, on Riečna Street near the River Danube. It's easily accessible by:

- Walking: If you're in the city center, it's about a 10-minute walk from the Main Square (Hlavné námestie).
- Tram: You can take tram line 4 or tram line 1, getting off at the Karadžičova station, a short walk from the gallery.

Cost (as of 2025):

- General Admission: €6
- Concessions (students, seniors): €3
- Children under 15: Free
- Free Entry: On Sundays, admission is free to all visitors.

From Anna, an Art Lover:

"I love the Slovak National Gallery. It's a quiet, elegant place where I can appreciate the depth of Slovak art. The medieval art section always fascinates me. It's a nice contrast to the more modern art exhibitions they host, which I enjoy as well. The gallery's location by the river also makes it a pleasant place to visit."

From Martin, a Local Resident:

"The Slovak National Gallery is one of my favorite places to visit when I have friends in town. It's got such a variety of art, and the building itself is beautiful. I also love the fact that entry is free on Sundays. It makes it an easy choice for a Sunday afternoon outing, especially if the weather isn't great."

Kunsthalle Bratislava: A Local's Perspective

Kunsthalle Bratislava is a modern art gallery located in the heart of the city, offering a space for contemporary art exhibitions, including painting, sculpture, installation art, and multimedia projects. Housed in a beautifully restored industrial building, Kunsthalle has become one of the leading contemporary art venues in Bratislava. It's a place where cutting-edge art meets thought-provoking concepts, and visitors can explore both Slovak and international artistic trends.

Highlights:

- The gallery features a rotating program of exhibitions, focusing on modern and contemporary artists.

- Kunsthalle hosts interactive art installations that often engage the viewer in unique and innovative ways.
- The venue also organizes art talks, workshops, and events designed to bring art to the community.
- The industrial architecture of the building itself is a major attraction, combining historical charm with a modern artistic atmosphere.

How to Get There:

Kunsthalle Bratislava is located just 5 minutes from the city center, near the Old Market Hall (Stará Tržnica). It's easily accessible by:

- Walking: The gallery is about a 10-minute walk from Main Square (Hlavné námestie).
- Tram: You can take tram lines 4 or 1 to the Karadžičova stop, which is only a few minutes away on foot from the gallery.

Cost (as of 2025):

- General Admission: €4
- Concessions (students, seniors): €2
- Free Entry: On the first Wednesday of every month, admission is free.

From Eva, a Contemporary Art Fan:

"I visit Kunsthalle every time there's a new exhibition. I really enjoy how they feature cutting-edge art that's always pushing boundaries. The space itself is incredible, with high ceilings and open areas that make the art feel even more expansive. I always feel inspired after leaving!"

From Jakub, a Local Resident:

"Kunsthalle is a hidden gem. It's one of my favorite places to spend a quiet afternoon. The interactive exhibits are always fascinating, and it's a great place to bring friends who are into contemporary art. It's also affordable, especially since entry is free on the first Wednesday of each month!"

Nedbalka Gallery: A Local's Perspective

Nedbalka Gallery is a modern art gallery in Bratislava, dedicated to showcasing Slovak art from the 20th century to the present. Housed in a charming, multi-level building with a striking open design, the gallery presents a unique and immersive experience. Its exhibitions feature a mix of paintings, sculptures, and installations by some of the most renowned Slovak artists, alongside innovative contemporary works. The gallery is a must-visit for art lovers who want to explore the depth of Slovak modern art.

Highlights:

- Permanent Collection focusing on Slovak modern art from the early 20th century to contemporary works.
- The gallery's unique architecture with open spaces and suspended platforms enhances the experience of viewing the art.
- Temporary exhibitions regularly highlight both Slovak and international contemporary artists.
- The intimate atmosphere makes it easy to fully immerse in the artwork without large crowds.

How to Get There:

Nedbalka Gallery is located just a short walk from Bratislava's Main Square (Hlavné námestie), making it easy to access by foot.

- Walking: From the Main Square, it's only a 5-minute walk to the gallery.
- Tram: You can also take tram line 4 and get off at the Zochova stop, which is about a 3-minute walk away.

Cost (as of 2025):

- General Admission: €4
- Concessions (students, seniors): €2
- Free Entry: On Sundays, admission is free for all visitors.

From Katarína, an Art Enthusiast:

"Nedbalka is one of my favorite galleries in Bratislava. The space itself is beautiful, and I love how it brings Slovak art to life with its clever use of architecture. Every time I visit, I discover something new—whether it's a modern installation or a piece by a classical Slovak artist."

From Tomáš, a Local Resident:

"I love the peaceful atmosphere of Nedbalka. It's not as crowded as some of the bigger galleries, and you really get a chance to appreciate the art. Plus, it's always nice to pop by on a Sunday when the entry is free—such a good way to spend a relaxing afternoon!"

Theaters:

Slovak National Theatre: A Local's Perspective

The Slovak National Theatre (Slovenské národné divadlo) is one of the most prestigious cultural institutions in Slovakia, offering a wide variety of performing arts, including opera, ballet, and drama. Located in the heart of Bratislava, this iconic venue is known for its grand architecture, which combines historical and modern elements. It regularly hosts performances by some of the country's most talented actors, musicians, and dancers, making it a must-visit for anyone interested in Slovakia's rich theatrical and cultural traditions.

Highlights:

- The theatre offers a variety of performances, from classic plays to modern dramas, ballet performances, and opera productions.
- The grand building itself is an architectural gem with a beautiful interior, featuring luxurious seating and impressive stages.
- The Slovak National Theatre is home to the Slovak National Opera and Ballet, which regularly stage world-class productions.
- There's a café and restaurant in the building, perfect for enjoying a meal or a drink before or after a performance.

How to Get There:

The Slovak National Theatre is located in the city center, just a short walk from the Main Square (Hlavné námestie).

- Walking: It's a 5-minute walk from the Main Square to the theatre.
- Tram: You can take tram line 4 or tram line 1, getting off at the Karadžičova or Zochova stops, both a few minutes' walk from the theatre.

Cost (as of 2025):

- Tickets for Drama: €10-€25, depending on the performance and seat location.
- Opera and Ballet Tickets: €15-€50, with higher prices for premium seats.
- Concessions: Discounts are available for students, seniors, and children, typically around 20%-30% off regular ticket prices.

From Lucia, a Theatre Lover:

"The Slovak National Theatre is the perfect place to experience high-quality performances. I especially love the ballet performances—they're always so graceful and beautifully choreographed. The venue itself is stunning, and I always enjoy spending a night out at the theatre with friends."

From Ján, a Local Resident:

"I've seen so many different performances here—from classic operas to contemporary plays. The atmosphere is always amazing, and the staff is very professional. I also appreciate how easy it is to get there from the city center—whether I walk or take the tram, it's just a short trip."

Arena Theatre: A Local's Perspective

Arena Theatre (Divadlo Arena) is one of Bratislava's most dynamic and intimate venues, known for its modern, experimental theatre performances. The theatre focuses on innovative plays, offering everything from contemporary dramas to experimental works and avant-garde productions. With its modern design and unique performances, Arena Theatre provides a more intimate experience than larger venues, making it a favorite among locals who appreciate cutting-edge theatre.

Highlights:

- Arena Theatre is known for its avant-garde performances that often push boundaries and challenge traditional theatre formats.
- It regularly hosts Slovak and international artists, with a mix of contemporary dramas and experimental performances.
- The venue is small, creating an intimate and engaging atmosphere that allows the audience to feel closer to the actors and the performance.
- Arena also offers a varied program with theatre festivals and special guest performances.

How to Get There:

Arena Theatre is located in the city center, near Karadžičova Street, just a short walk from the Main Square (Hlavné námestie).

- Walking: The theatre is a 10-minute walk from the Main Square.
- Tram: You can take tram lines 4 or 1, getting off at the Zochova stop, which is a few minutes away from the theatre.

Cost (as of 2025):

- General Admission: €10-€20, depending on the performance and seat selection.
- Concessions (students, seniors): Around €5-€12.
- Special Events/Festivals: Prices may vary, but typically range between €15-€30 for special performances or guest shows.

From Martina, a Theatre Enthusiast:

Arena Theatre is where you can see something really unique. I've attended several experimental plays, and they always leave me thinking. The atmosphere is more intimate than larger venues, so it's a special experience each time. I love how they bring in international artists too."

From Michal, a Local Resident:

"I enjoy Arena Theatre because it's not your typical theatre. The performances are often bold and original, and I like that the theatre isn't afraid to take risks. It's a great spot to enjoy an evening of cultural exploration, and the ticket prices are very reasonable."

Old Market Hall (Stará Tržnica): A Local's Perspective

The Old Market Hall (Stará Tržnica) is one of Bratislava's most iconic historical buildings, originally built in the early 20th century. Located in the heart of the city, it serves as a vibrant space for a variety of events, markets, and cultural activities. The building itself is a charming blend of Art Nouveau architecture and modern use, hosting everything from farmers' markets to craft fairs and concerts. It's a lively spot where locals gather to shop, socialize, and enjoy the city's dynamic atmosphere.

Highlights:

- The Old Market Hall hosts regular farmers' markets with fresh produce, handmade goods, and local specialties.
- It also features a range of events such as art exhibitions, live music performances, and food festivals.
- The beautiful architecture of the building is a highlight in itself, with its open layout and decorative touches.
- The hall's central location makes it a great stop for anyone exploring the city center, and there's a café inside where you can relax after shopping or sightseeing.

How to Get There:

The Old Market Hall is located just a 5-minute walk from Bratislava's Main Square (Hlavné námestie).

- Walking: From the Main Square, it's just a short stroll to the market.
- Tram: You can also take tram lines 4, 1, or 5, and get off at Karadžičova stop, which is just a few minutes' walk to the building.

Cost (as of 2025):

- Entry: Most events are free of charge, though some special events or markets may charge a small entry fee (typically €2-€5).
- Markets: There's no entry fee to visit the regular markets, but if you're shopping, prices vary depending on what you buy.
- Events/Concerts: Depending on the performance, tickets generally range from €5-€15.

From Lenka, a Market Regular:

"I love visiting the Old Market Hall on weekends. The farmers' market always has fresh local produce, and I enjoy picking up some homemade pastries. The place has such a lively vibe, and I always find something interesting to take home."

From Peter, a Local Resident:

"The Old Market Hall is a fantastic spot for a casual afternoon out. It's close to everything, and I often pop in to check out the events or grab a coffee. The building is gorgeous, and there's always something going on, whether it's a craft fair or a concert."

Gorila.sk Urban Space: A Local's Perspective

Gorila.sk Urban Space is a trendy cultural venue in Bratislava, known for its creative atmosphere and focus on music, film, and literature. It's a vibrant space that brings together locals and visitors to enjoy everything from live concerts to film screenings and book launches. The venue also doubles as a café and bookstore, making it a great place to relax, browse, and enjoy a drink while soaking in the local cultural scene.

Highlights:

- Live music events featuring local and international artists, spanning genres from indie rock to electronic music.
- A film screening room where independent films and documentaries are shown regularly.
- A bookstore that focuses on Slovak literature, art books, and novels, creating a space where you can discover new reads.
- A cozy café offering great coffee, snacks, and a comfortable place to hang out before or after an event.

How to Get There:

Gorila.sk Urban Space is centrally located in Bratislava's Old Town, close to many cultural landmarks.

- Walking: It's about a 5-minute walk from Bratislava's Main Square (Hlavné námestie).
- Tram: You can take tram lines 4 or 5, getting off at Zochova or Karadžičova stops, both just a short walk from the venue.

Cost (as of 2025):

- General Admission for Events: Typically €5-€15, depending on the performance or screening.
- Bookstore Prices: Vary depending on the book, but expect to pay €5-€20 for most titles.

- Café: Drinks and snacks range from €2-€5.

From Lucia, a Regular Visitor:

"I love hanging out at Gorila.sk Urban Space. The atmosphere is always relaxed, and there's always something interesting going on, whether it's a small gig or a film screening. I also love browsing the bookstore—they have some great selections of local and international books."

From Marek, a Local Resident:

"Gorila.sk is my go-to place for a casual night out. I've seen some fantastic concerts here, and the café is perfect for grabbing a coffee with friends before the event. The space has such a cool vibe, and it's great that they focus on local talent and independent art.

Music Venues:

Reduta Concert Hall: A Local's Perspective

Reduta Concert Hall (Slovenská filharmónia) is one of Bratislava's premier classical music venues, renowned for its elegant architecture and superb acoustics. Located on the banks of the River Danube, Reduta is home to the Slovak Philharmonic Orchestra and hosts a wide range of classical concerts, from symphonies to chamber music recitals. The building itself is a historical gem, offering an intimate yet grand setting for music lovers.

Highlights:

- The Slovak Philharmonic Orchestra performs here regularly, showcasing both classic and contemporary compositions.
- International guest artists and orchestras also perform, making it a top venue for world-class music performances.
- The concert hall's acoustics are renowned, ensuring a high-quality listening experience for every performance.
- The historic building offers a beautiful interior, with a classic, elegant atmosphere that adds to the charm of the venue.

How to Get There:

Reduta Concert Hall is located in Bratislava's city center, just a short walk from the Main Square (Hlavné námestie).

- Walking: It's only a 5-minute walk from the Main Square along the Danube riverbank.
- Tram: You can take tram lines 4 or 5 and get off at Karadžičova or Zochova stops, which are a short walk from the concert hall.

Cost (as of 2025):

- Tickets for Concerts: €10-€40, depending on the performance and seating choice.
- Student/Senior Discounts: Typically €5-€20 for discounted tickets.
- Special Concerts: Prices may vary for special performances or guest artists, often ranging from €15-€50.

From Jana, a Classical Music Enthusiast:

"Reduta is my favorite place to enjoy live classical music. The acoustics are perfect, and it's such a beautiful, historic building. Whether I'm attending a Slovak Philharmonic concert or a guest performance, I always feel transported by the music."

From Peter, a Local Resident:

"I attend concerts at Reduta whenever I can. The experience is so much more intimate than larger venues, and the acoustics make the music sound incredible. It's a place that really highlights the rich cultural life of Bratislava."

The Philharmonic Hall: A Local's Perspective

The Philharmonic Hall (Filharmónia Bratislava) is a key cultural venue in Bratislava, renowned for its stunning classical music performances and exceptional acoustics. The hall hosts a variety of concerts, from orchestral works to chamber music, offering an intimate atmosphere for lovers of classical music. It is home to the Bratislava Symphony Orchestra and often features international artists, making it one of the top spots for enjoying high-quality performances in the city.

Highlights:

The Bratislava Symphony Orchestra performs regularly, offering a broad range of classical music from baroque to contemporary pieces.

The hall's acoustics are finely tuned for classical performances, ensuring an exceptional auditory experience for all visitors.

The venue regularly hosts guest performances by renowned international musicians and orchestras.

The elegant design of the hall and its rich history add to the cultural significance of attending an event here.

How to Get There:

- The Philharmonic Hall is centrally located, making it easily accessible from Bratislava's city center.
- Walking: It's about a 10-minute walk from Main Square (Hlavné námestie) along Karadžičova Street.

- Tram: Take tram lines 1, 4, or 5 and get off at the Zochova stop, which is a short walk from the hall.

Cost (as of 2025):

- Concert Tickets: Prices typically range from €10-€30, depending on the performance and seating.
- Discounts: There are discounted tickets for students and seniors, generally ranging from €5-€15.
- Special Events: Prices for special performances or guest musicians can be slightly higher, around €20-€50.

From Anna, a Classical Music Aficionado:

"I love visiting the Philharmonic Hall. The acoustics are phenomenal, and it's always such a joy to hear the Bratislava Symphony Orchestra live. The intimate setting makes every concert feel special, and the atmosphere is just perfect for classical music."

From Martin, a Local Resident:

"The Philharmonic Hall is one of the best places to experience live classical music in Bratislava. The concerts are always top-notch, and I love the feeling of being so close to the musicians. It's a hidden gem in the city's music scene."

Ateliér Babylon: A Local's Perspective

Ateliér Babylon is a unique cultural space in Bratislava, known for its art exhibitions, creative workshops, and alternative events. It's a place where both local artists and emerging talents showcase their works. The venue offers a relaxed and artistic environment, perfect for those who appreciate contemporary art, experimental projects, and a community-focused space. It also hosts a variety of performances, theatre events, and film screenings, making it a hub for the city's creative scene.

Highlights:

- Ateliér Babylon hosts regular art exhibitions, featuring visual art, photography, and installations by Slovak and international artists.
- The space is known for its interactive workshops that encourage visitors to engage with art, whether through painting, sculpture, or crafts.
- It also offers cultural events such as theatre performances, live music, and independent film screenings.
- The venue provides a unique, laid-back atmosphere, where visitors can enjoy art in an informal setting while socializing with like-minded individuals.

How to Get There:

Ateliér Babylon is conveniently located in Bratislava's Old Town.

- Walking: It's about a 10-minute walk from Main Square (Hlavné námestie).

- Tram: You can take tram lines 1 or 4, getting off at the Karadžičova or Zochova stop, both a few minutes' walk from the venue.

Cost (as of 2025):

- Exhibition Entry: Typically €2-€5, depending on the exhibit.
- Workshops/Events: Prices vary based on the event, generally ranging from €5-€15.
- Special Events: For larger performances or unique screenings, tickets may cost between €10-€20.

From Eva, an Art Lover:

"Ateliér Babylon is one of my favorite places to visit. I love how the exhibitions are always fresh and different—there's always something new to explore. Plus, the workshops are so much fun. It's a great way to get creative and meet other people who love art."

From Jakub, a Local Resident:

"I come to Ateliér Babylon to relax and enjoy the artistic vibe. It's a place that really supports local talent, and I always enjoy the intimate feel of the events. Whether I'm checking out a new art exhibit or watching a small play, it's always a great experience."

Majestic Music Club: A Local's Perspective

Majestic Music Club is one of Bratislava's premier venues for live music, particularly known for its electronic music scene. Located in the heart of the city, this club has become a favorite spot for locals and visitors looking to enjoy vibrant nightlife and high-energy performances. With its modern sound system, intimate atmosphere, and diverse lineup of DJs and live acts, it's the place to be for anyone wanting to experience Bratislava's music scene.

Highlights:

- Majestic Music Club hosts a variety of live performances, with a focus on electronic music, house, and techno genres.
- The venue also features international DJs, along with local talent, offering something for everyone in the electronic music community.
- The modern sound and lighting system creates an immersive experience, making it one of the best places in Bratislava to enjoy music.
- It's known for its laid-back vibe—perfect for those who want to dance the night away or enjoy live music in a more intimate setting.

How to Get There:

Majestic Music Club is located in the city center, making it easy to reach from most parts of Bratislava.

- Walking: It's about a 5-minute walk from Main Square (Hlavné námestie).
- Tram: You can take tram lines 1 or 4, getting off at the Karadžičova stop, which is just a few minutes' walk from the club.

Cost (as of 2025):

- Entry: Typically €5-€15, depending on the event or DJ performance.
- Special Events: Prices for larger shows or special guest DJs can be higher, usually around €20-€30.
- Drinks: Expect to pay €2-€5 for drinks, depending on your choice.

From Jana, a Nightlife Enthusiast:

"Majestic is my go-to spot when I want to dance and have a great time. The music is always top-notch, and the atmosphere is amazing. It's not too big, so you get that intimate feel even when it's packed. I've seen some awesome DJs here!"

From Adam, a Local Resident:

"I've been to Majestic many times. The sound system is incredible, and the crowd is always fun. Whether it's a local DJ or someone more famous, the nights here are always unforgettable. It's definitely one of the best places for electronic music in Bratislava."

Chapter 8. Where to Eat and Drink

Traditional Slovak Cuisine: Must-Try Dishes

Bryndzové Halušky: A Local's Perspective

Bryndzové Halušky is considered Slovakia's national dish, a beloved comfort food that combines soft, potato dumplings (halušky) with brined sheep cheese (bryndza) and topped with crispy bacon or slanina. It's a dish that represents traditional Slovak cuisine at its finest, hearty and rich in flavor. Often served in a large portion, it's perfect for sharing among friends or family, and it's found in most Slovak restaurants.

Highlights:

- The bryndza gives the dish its distinctive creamy and slightly tangy flavor, making it unlike anything else you'll taste.
- The potato dumplings are soft and comforting, a true staple of Slovak food.
- It's often accompanied by a side of sour cream and crispy bacon, adding texture and a savory kick.
- Perfect for lunch or dinner, it's a filling and satisfying dish, loved by locals and visitors alike.

Cost (as of 2025):

- Average Price: €7-€12 for a full portion at most restaurants.
- Sharing for Two: The dish is quite filling, so sharing a portion between two people is common, costing around €10-€15 for both.

From Mária, a Slovak Local:

"Bryndzové Halušky is my comfort food—whenever I'm in the mood for something filling and traditional, this is it. The rich taste of bryndza mixed with the soft halušky and crispy bacon is unbeatable. It's something we always share when eating with friends or family."

From Tomáš, a Local Resident:

"I grew up eating Bryndzové Halušky. It's the kind of dish that makes you feel right at home. I love it on a chilly day, and no matter where I go in Slovakia, I always compare how others prepare it. It's always delicious and hearty."

Kapustnica: A Local's Perspective

Kapustnica is a hearty Slovak sauerkraut soup that holds a special place in local cuisine, especially during the Christmas season. Made from fermented cabbage (kapusta), smoked meats, and mushrooms, it's a flavorful and tangy dish often served with a slice of rye bread or fried bread on the side. The soup can be adjusted with various ingredients like sausage or even dried plums, adding depth and sweetness to the savory broth. It's comforting, filling, and perfect for the cold winter months.

Highlights:

- Fermented cabbage gives Kapustnica its unique sour flavor, a defining characteristic of the dish.
- Smoked meats like sausage and ham provide a rich, smoky taste that balances the tanginess of the cabbage.
- It's commonly enjoyed during the holiday season, but many locals enjoy it year-round, especially in colder weather.
- Often served with bread or dumplings to make it a more complete meal.

Cost (as of 2025):

- Average Price: €5-€9 for a bowl of Kapustnica at most restaurants.
- For Two People: A shared portion or two individual bowls will typically cost around €10-€18.

From Eva, a Slovak Local:

"Kapustnica is a must-have during the holidays for us, but honestly, I could eat it any time of the year. The smoky meats combined with the tangy cabbage make it feel so comforting, especially in winter. It's the perfect soup to warm you up!"

From Jozef, a Local Resident:

"Kapustnica is something I grew up with. It's the kind of soup that reminds me of family gatherings and celebrations. I love it with plenty of sausage, and it's perfect with a slice of fresh bread. Whenever I see it on the menu, I can't resist!"

Zemiakové Placky: A Local's Perspective

Zemiakové Placky are delicious potato pancakes that are crispy on the outside and soft on the inside, often served as a snack or side dish in Slovakia. Made from grated potatoes, flour, eggs, and seasoning, these pancakes are typically fried to golden perfection. They can be enjoyed plain or topped with garlic, sour cream, or even a sprinkle of cheese for extra flavor. A beloved comfort food, Zemiakové Placky are especially popular in family gatherings and are frequently seen at festivals or street food stalls.

Highlights:

- Crispy on the outside, soft and flavorful on the inside.
- Can be served with a variety of toppings like sour cream, cheese, or garlic for added taste.
- Often eaten as a side dish, but they are filling enough to enjoy as a light meal or snack.
- Simple yet satisfying, a perfect comfort food loved by locals of all ages.

Cost (as of 2025):

- Average Price: €3-€6 for a serving of Zemiakové Placky at most restaurants or food stalls.
- For Two People: Sharing a portion of Zemiakové Placky typically costs around €6-€10.

From Ivana, a Slovak Local:

"Zemiakové Placky are a childhood favorite for me. I love them with sour cream on top—it's such a simple dish, but so comforting. Whether I'm at a festival or making them at home, they always hit the spot."

From Marek, a Local Resident:

"Whenever I'm craving something quick and delicious, Zemiakové Placky are my go-to. I like them with a little garlic and cheese on top, and they're perfect with a cold drink. It's the kind of food that makes me feel at home."

Guláš: A Local's Perspective

Guláš is a hearty and flavorful beef stew that's a staple in Slovak cuisine. Originally inspired by Hungarian goulash, it's made with tender chunks of beef, onions, paprika, and other seasonings, creating a rich and savory dish. The stew is often served with bread, dumplings, or potatoes, and sometimes garnished with a dollop of sour cream. Whether enjoyed in a rustic Slovak pub or at a family dinner, Guláš is a comforting and satisfying dish, especially popular during colder months.

Highlights:

- The beef is slow-cooked to tenderness, allowing the flavors of paprika and onion to meld together perfectly.
- Often served with dumplings or bread to soak up the flavorful broth.
- It's a filling dish, making it perfect for lunch or dinner.
- Versatile—while the classic version uses beef, some variations include pork or venison.

Cost (as of 2025):

- Average Price: €7-€12 for a bowl of Guláš, depending on the restaurant and portion size.
- For Two People: Ordering two bowls will typically cost around €14-€24, depending on location and toppings.

From Lucia, a Slovak Local:

"Guláš is a dish I associate with family meals and gatherings. The rich flavors of paprika and the tender beef always make me feel warm and satisfied. It's a great dish to share with friends or family, especially when served with dumplings!"

From Peter, a Local Resident:

"I grew up eating Guláš on Sundays, and it's still one of my favorites. The slow-cooked meat and the paprika make it so flavorful. Whether I'm at a pub or cooking it at home, it's always a filling and comforting meal."

Best Restaurants for Every Budget

Slovenská Reštaurácia: A Local's Perspective

Slovenská Reštaurácia is a charming and cozy restaurant that offers an authentic taste of Slovak cuisine in a traditional setting. Located in the heart of Bratislava, it specializes in classic Slovak dishes, making it a favorite among locals and tourists alike who want to experience the true flavors of Slovakia. From hearty Bryndzové Halušky (potato dumplings with sheep cheese) to tender Sviečková (beef with creamy sauce), this restaurant brings the warmth and comfort of Slovak home cooking to your table. The atmosphere is warm, rustic, and inviting, with wooden accents and traditional décor that add to the experience.

What They Have to Offer:

- Traditional Slovak Dishes: Enjoy authentic dishes like Bryndzové Halušky, Kapustnica (sauerkraut soup), Zemiakové Placky (potato pancakes), and Guláš (stew), all made with fresh, locally sourced ingredients.
- Slovak Beverages: The restaurant also offers a selection of local wines, Slovak beers, and homemade fruit spirits such as slivovica (plum brandy) to pair perfectly with your meal.
- Homemade Desserts: Don't miss out on their sweet offerings like Koláče (traditional Slovak pastries) or Šúľance (sweet dumplings with poppy seeds).
- Family-Friendly: The cozy, welcoming atmosphere makes it ideal for family meals or casual gatherings.

How to Get There:

Slovenská Reštaurácia is centrally located, making it easily accessible from the Old Town.

- Walking: It's about a 5-10 minute walk from Main Square (Hlavné námestie), just follow the charming streets towards the Michalská Brána (Michael's Gate).
- Tram: You can take tram lines 1, 4, or 5 and get off at the Karadžičova stop, which is just a short walk from the restaurant.

Cost (as of 2025):

- Average Price: €8-€15 for a main dish.
- For Two People: Expect to pay around €20-€30 for two main courses, a shared appetizer, and drinks.

From Jana, a Local Resident:

"Slovenská Reštaurácia is where I always take guests who want to try real Slovak food. The dishes are always authentic and delicious. The Bryndzové Halušky here are the best in the city, and the Kapustnica is just like my grandmother's! It's a perfect spot for a cozy meal with family or friends."

From Martin, a Local Resident:

"This place has a really welcoming atmosphere, and the food is spot on. I love the traditional Slovak meals they serve, especially the Sviečková. It's perfect for when I'm craving something hearty and comforting. The service is friendly too, and I always feel at home here."

Modrá Hviezda: A Local's Perspective

Modrá Hviezda is one of Bratislava's most beloved fine dining spots, known for its stunning atmosphere and refined Slovak cuisine. Situated in a charming historical building just a short walk from the city center, this restaurant combines a rich traditional Slovak menu with a modern touch. Its interior blends classic and contemporary design, offering a cozy yet sophisticated vibe. Whether you're celebrating a special occasion or simply want to experience a top-tier meal, Modrá Hviezda offers an unforgettable dining experience.

What They Have to Offer:

- Traditional Slovak Dishes with a Twist: Modrá Hviezda takes classic Slovak flavors and presents them in an elevated way. Popular dishes include Sviečková (beef in creamy vegetable sauce), Kapustnica (sauerkraut soup), and Bryndzové Halušky (potato dumplings with sheep cheese). Expect fresh, high-quality ingredients and creative presentations.
- Local and Seasonal Ingredients: The restaurant emphasizes locally sourced, fresh ingredients, making sure the flavors reflect the changing seasons.
- Slovak Wines and Spirits: Modrá Hviezda offers a great selection of Slovak wines that pair perfectly with their dishes, along with homemade fruit spirits, like slivovica (plum brandy), for those looking to try something local.
- Elegant Dining Experience: The ambiance is sophisticated, with dim lighting, soft music, and attentive service—perfect for an intimate dinner or special occasion.

How to Get There:

Modrá Hviezda is located in the Old Town of Bratislava, close to some of the city's iconic landmarks.

- Walking: It's about a 5-minute walk from Main Square (Hlavné námestie). Head towards the Primate's Palace, and you'll find it on a quaint street just around the corner.
- Tram: You can take tram lines 1 or 4, getting off at the Karadžičova stop. From there, it's a 5-minute walk to the restaurant.

Cost (as of 2025):

- Average Price: €15-€25 for a main dish.
- For Two People: Expect to pay around €40-€60 for two main courses, an appetizer, drinks, and dessert.

From Lucia, a Local Resident:

"Modrá Hviezda is a perfect spot when you want to indulge in Slovak cuisine but with a touch of elegance. I've come here for several family celebrations and it never disappoints. The Sviečková is amazing, and the ambiance is always just right for a special night out. It's one of the places I recommend to friends who want a memorable experience in Bratislava."

From Ján, a Local Resident:

"I love Modrá Hviezda for its combination of traditional flavors and modern presentation. It's not your typical touristy restaurant, and the food is always fantastic. The staff is friendly and attentive, and I appreciate how they focus on local ingredients. It's a great place for a nice evening out in the heart of the city."

Savoy Restaurant: A Local's Perspective

Savoy Restaurant is one of Bratislava's most renowned fine dining spots, offering a blend of classic elegance and modern sophistication. Located in a beautifully restored building, it exudes a sense of grandeur with its art deco interior, high ceilings, and luxurious ambiance. The restaurant is known for its exquisite European and Slovak cuisine, with an emphasis on refined presentation and exceptional service. Whether you're in the mood for a relaxed meal or a special celebration, Savoy provides the perfect atmosphere for any occasion.

What They Have to Offer:

- European and Slovak Fusion: The menu at Savoy seamlessly blends traditional Slovak ingredients with international culinary techniques. You can enjoy dishes such as filet of beef with a rich sauce, roasted duck, and delicate fish fillets. Their Bryndzové Halušky (potato dumplings with sheep cheese) also appears with a creative twist.
- Seasonal Ingredients: Savoy prides itself on using the freshest seasonal produce to create beautifully presented dishes that celebrate local flavors.

- Sophisticated Wine Pairings: The restaurant offers an extensive selection of both Slovak and international wines. Their wine list is carefully curated to complement each dish, with knowledgeable staff offering excellent recommendations.
- Elegant Desserts: Don't skip dessert—Savoy offers decadent sweets such as chocolate mousse, fruit tarts, and Slovak-inspired pastries. The desserts are as refined as the rest of the menu.

How to Get There:

Savoy Restaurant is centrally located in Bratislava, making it easy to reach from several key points in the city.

- Walking: It's located just a 5-10 minute walk from Main Square (Hlavné námestie). Walk towards Karadžičova Street, and you'll find the restaurant nestled in the vicinity of Špitálska street.
- Tram: You can take tram lines 1 or 4, get off at Karadžičova, and from there, it's about a 5-minute walk to the restaurant.

Cost (as of 2025):

- Average Price: €20-€35 for a main dish.
- For Two People: A meal with starters, mains, dessert, and drinks will typically cost around €50-€80.

From Eva, a Local Resident:

"Savoy is where I go when I want to feel special. The ambiance is so elegant, and the food is always top-notch. I love their creative take on traditional Slovak dishes—like their Bryndzové Halušky, which is just amazing. It's a perfect spot for a romantic dinner or a celebration."

From Peter, a Local Resident:

"I've been to Savoy a few times, and every experience has been outstanding. The menu is a beautiful mix of Slovak classics and European cuisine. I particularly enjoy the duck dishes, and the wine selection never disappoints. If you want something upscale in the heart of Bratislava, this is definitely the place to go."

Houdini Restaurant: A Local's Perspective

Houdini Restaurant is a unique, stylish dining destination in the heart of Bratislava, known for its elegant atmosphere and modern take on Slovak and international cuisine. Located near the city center, this chic restaurant offers a sophisticated yet approachable dining experience, perfect for those looking for a memorable meal in a sleek setting. The interior features a mix of contemporary design and subtle nods to historical charm, making it a popular choice for both locals and tourists seeking a fine dining experience.

What They Have to Offer:

- Modern Slovak Cuisine: Houdini offers a creative menu that blends traditional Slovak flavors with modern techniques. You'll find dishes like wild boar with potato purée, beef tartare, and a variety of fresh fish preparations. The menu constantly evolves, with seasonal specials to keep things fresh.
- International Influences: While it focuses on Slovak ingredients, the restaurant adds an international twist to many of its dishes, making it a great place for food lovers looking for something a little different.
- Exquisite Presentation: Every dish is beautifully plated, showcasing a careful attention to detail. The combination of taste and artful presentation makes each meal a visual and culinary treat.
- Fine Wines & Cocktails: Houdini boasts an extensive wine list, focusing on Slovak wines alongside international options. Their signature cocktails are also popular, offering a unique way to begin your meal or relax afterward.

How to Get There:

Houdini Restaurant is conveniently located near the city center, making it easy to reach by foot or public transport.

- Walking: It's about a 5-10 minute walk from Hlavné námestie (Main Square). From there, simply walk towards Špitálska Street or Karadžičova Street, and you'll find the restaurant along a quiet, atmospheric street.
- Tram: You can hop on tram lines 1, 4, or 5, and get off at the Karadžičova stop, which is just a 5-minute walk from the restaurant.

Cost (as of 2025):

- Average Price: €18-€30 for a main dish.
- For Two People: A meal with starters, main courses, dessert, and drinks will cost around €50-€70.

From Mária, a Local Resident:

"I love Houdini because it's where traditional Slovak cuisine meets modern flair. The food is always fresh, and the atmosphere is so stylish and relaxed. It's a great place for a special dinner with friends or a romantic evening. The beef tartare here is one of the best I've ever had!"

From Tomáš, a Local Resident:

"Houdini is one of those places that never disappoints. The menu always surprises me—there's something about the way they blend local ingredients with international techniques that makes it unique. I've been here multiple times and every dish feels like a work of art. It's definitely one of my top choices when I want a special dining experience in Bratislava."

Slovak Drinks: Wine, Beer, and Liquor

Slovakia has a rich tradition of beverages that reflect its deep cultural history and passion for good flavors. Whether you're in the mood for a refreshing beer, a fine wine, or a distinctive local liquor, Slovakia offers a variety of drinks that will appeal to every taste. Here's an overview of the most popular Slovak drinks you should try.

Slovak Wine

Slovakia is home to a number of wine regions, with the Small Carpathian wine region (Malokarpatská vinohradnícka oblasť) and the Tokaj region being the most renowned. Slovak wines are diverse, from light whites to rich reds, and often feature indigenous varieties.

- Popular Wines:
    - Veltlínske Zelené (Green Veltliner): A popular white wine in Slovakia, known for its crisp, fresh taste with hints of citrus and green apple.
    - Rizling (Riesling): A well-known white wine, often with a balance of sweetness and acidity.
    - Frankovka Modrá (Blaufränkisch): A native red wine variety that's rich and smooth, often with berry flavors.
    - Tokaj: A sweet wine from the famous Tokaj region, known for its Tokaji Aszú wines, which are made from dried grapes and have a sweet, honeyed flavor.
- Cost:
    - A glass of Slovak wine will typically cost around €3-€5 at most restaurants or bars.
    - A bottle of Slovak wine at a wine shop may range from €8-€20, depending on the quality and region.

Slovak Beer

Beer is an integral part of Slovak culture, and the country is home to some exceptional brews. Slovak beer tends to be light and refreshing, making it perfect for the country's social and outdoor gatherings. Slovaks pride themselves on their beer and have several well-established breweries.

- Popular Slovak Beers:
    - Šariš: A widely consumed lager known for its crisp taste and smooth finish. It's one of Slovakia's largest beer brands.
    - Zlatý Bažant: Another popular lager, often served in many pubs and restaurants across the country.
    - Corgoň: A slightly stronger lager that is popular in the country's pubs and also widely available in international markets.
    - Kelt: A premium lager known for its richer flavor, often slightly sweeter than the others.
    - Craft Beers: Slovakia has seen a rise in craft breweries in recent years, with beers like Kreator and Pilsner-style craft beers becoming increasingly popular.
- Cost:

- A pint of Slovak beer at a local pub will usually cost €2-€4.
- A bottle of local beer in a store can range from €0.80-€1.50, with craft beers being a little more expensive at €2-€4 per bottle.

Slovak Liquor

Slovak spirits are often enjoyed after a meal or during social gatherings. The most famous Slovak liquor is Borovička, a juniper-flavored spirit that is similar to gin but with a distinctly stronger taste.

- Popular Slovak Liquors:
    - Borovička: A traditional Slovak drink made from juniper berries, typically served as a digestif. It's often homemade and is considered a national drink in Slovakia.
    - Slivovica (Plum Brandy): A strong, fruity liquor made from plums. Slivovica is a favorite for celebratory moments, and many Slovaks even distill it themselves.
    - Tatratea: A famous herbal liqueur made from high mountain plants in the Tatra Mountains. It comes in several varieties, ranging from 27% to 72% alcohol, making it one of the strongest spirits available in Slovakia.
    - Trnkovica: A spirit made from sloes (a type of berry), it has a similar taste profile to Slivovica but is often a little sweeter.
- Cost:
    - A shot of Borovička or Slivovica at a bar will typically cost €2-€3.
    - Tatratea is usually priced at €3-€5 per shot in a bar, depending on the strength and location.

Cost Summary for Drinks (Approximate):

- Wine: €3-€5 for a glass, €8-€20 for a bottle.
- Beer: €2-€4 for a pint at a pub, €0.80-€1.50 for a bottle in a store.
- Liquor: €2-€5 for a shot of Borovička or Slivovica, €3-€5 for Tatratea.

From Lucia, a Local Resident:

"When I go out with friends, I usually order Borovička; it's such a great drink to enjoy with others. If you're a fan of beer, I recommend trying Zlatý Bažant; it's perfect for any occasion. And for wine lovers, Slovakia has some fantastic local options—especially Tokaj wine. It's a treat!"

From Peter, a Local Resident:

"Slovak beer is always my go-to, especially after a long day of work. I love visiting a local pub and having a pint of Šariš—it's refreshing and not too heavy. As for liquor, Slivovica is a classic for celebrations, and Tatratea is one of the most interesting drinks you'll find here—strong but smooth. Definitely give it a try!"

Chapter 9. Shopping and Souvenirs

Best Shopping Streets and Malls

Obchodná Street: A Local's Perspective

Obchodná Street is one of the most popular shopping destinations in Bratislava, known for its vibrant atmosphere and wide array of shops, cafes, and restaurants. The street is lined with a mix of high-end international brands, local boutiques, and quirky shops, offering something for everyone. Whether you're on the hunt for fashion, souvenirs, or simply enjoy window shopping, Obchodná Street is the place to be.

Important Highlights:

- Variety of Shops: From trendy clothing stores and shoe shops to bookstores and electronics stores, Obchodná Street has a little bit of everything. It's perfect for both casual shoppers and those looking for something more high-end.
- Cafes and Restaurants: Along with shopping, Obchodná also offers plenty of places to grab a coffee, lunch, or dinner. Local favorites like Café Mayer and Café Possonium line the street, providing a cozy break between shopping sessions.
- Street Performers and Local Art: On busy days, you'll likely come across street performers and local artists, adding a cultural touch to the area.
- Central Location: Obchodná Street is located in the heart of the city, making it a convenient starting point for exploring other areas of Bratislava, like the Old Town and the Slovak National Theatre.

How to Get There:

- Walking: If you're in Old Town, Obchodná Street is just a 5-minute walk from Main Square (Hlavné námestie). Simply walk towards Karadžičova Street, and you'll find it right in the middle of the city center.
- Tram: You can take tram line 1 or tram line 4, and get off at Karadžičova. From there, it's only a 3-minute walk to reach the street.

From Jana, a Local Resident:

"Obchodná Street is always bustling with activity, and I love walking down it when I need to pick up something new. I often stop for coffee at Café Mayer or grab a quick lunch before heading to the shops. It's great to see so many local stores mixed in with the international ones. It's my go-to shopping street!"

From Martin, a Local Resident:

"I visit Obchodná Street whenever I'm looking for a good mix of shops. Whether I'm looking for clothing, books, or just browsing around, it never disappoints. It's also nice to pop into one of the cafés for a break. The street is always full of life, and there's something special about shopping here, especially when there are street performances."

Panta Rhei: A Local's Perspective

Panta Rhei is one of Bratislava's most well-known bookstores, and it's a true haven for book lovers. Located along Obchodná Street, it offers a wide selection of books in multiple languages, from fiction and non-fiction to art and travel guides. With its cozy, inviting atmosphere, it's the perfect place to spend a few hours browsing, reading, or even enjoying a coffee.

Important Highlights:

- Extensive Book Collection: Panta Rhei is renowned for its extensive selection of both Slovak and international books. Whether you're into contemporary fiction, historical novels, or more niche topics like philosophy and art, you'll find something here.
- Books in Multiple Languages: While the focus is on Slovak literature, there's also a great variety of books in English, German, and other languages, making it an ideal spot for both locals and tourists.
- Friendly Atmosphere: The layout of the store is spacious, and the cozy ambiance makes it an enjoyable place to wander. The staff is always helpful, and there's no rush to make a purchase, so you can take your time discovering new titles.
- Café Corner: They have a small café inside, where you can enjoy a cup of coffee or tea while flipping through your latest find. It's a relaxed spot to unwind after a shopping trip or while taking a break from exploring the city.

How to Get There:

- Walking: Panta Rhei is located on Obchodná Street, so if you're already in the Old Town area, it's just a 5-minute walk from Main Square (Hlavné námestie). Walk down Obchodná Street, and you'll see it on your right.
- Tram: If you're using public transport, you can hop on tram lines 1 or 4, and get off at Karadžičova stop, which is only a 3-minute walk from the bookstore.

From Eva, a Local Resident:

"I come to Panta Rhei every time I'm looking for a new book to read. It's my favorite bookstore in Bratislava! I love how they have a great mix of local and international books. Plus, the coffee corner is such a great spot to relax and read a few pages."

From Lukas, a Local Resident:

"Panta Rhei is the place to go if you want to find a book in any language. They always have the newest releases, and I can spend hours just browsing. It's a perfect mix of culture and shopping for me. Whenever I'm in Obchodná Street, I always stop by."

Eurovea Shopping Mall: A Local's Perspective

Eurovea Shopping Mall is one of the most modern and upscale shopping centers in Bratislava, offering a perfect blend of luxury brands, local shops, and entertainment options. Situated along the Danube River, the mall offers not just shopping, but a stunning view of the water, making it a popular destination for locals and tourists alike.

Important Highlights:

- Variety of Shops: Eurovea boasts a wide selection of both international luxury brands (like H&M, Zara, and Lacoste) and local Slovak stores, catering to all tastes and budgets. It's the perfect place for shopping, whether you're looking for the latest fashion, electronics, or beauty products.
- Dining Options: The mall features a great variety of restaurants, cafes, and food stalls offering both local Slovak food and international cuisine. There's something for every craving, from a quick snack to a fine dining experience with views of the Danube.
- Entertainment: Beyond shopping, Eurovea also offers entertainment options, such as a cinema and occasional live events. The riverside promenade provides a great place to walk and relax, especially in the summer.
- Riverside Location: One of the highlights of Eurovea is its location right next to the Danube River, providing beautiful views of the water and the city. You can enjoy a peaceful walk along the river after your shopping spree.

How to Get There:

- Walking: Eurovea is just a 10-minute walk from Bratislava Old Town. Head toward the Danube River from Hlavné námestie (Main Square), and you'll easily find the mall along the waterfront.
- Tram: You can also take tram line 1 or tram line 4 and get off at the Eurovea stop. The mall is right next to the tram stop, making it easy to access.

From Petra, a Local Resident:

"Eurovea is my go-to spot when I want to shop in comfort. The stores are great, and I love sitting by the river afterward with a coffee. It's just so relaxing, and there's always something happening here. I also enjoy the fact that you can find both luxury and affordable brands."

From Martin, a Local Resident:

"Eurovea is not just for shopping; it's an experience. I come here not only for the stores but for the views. It's lovely to take a walk along the river and then grab lunch at one of the many restaurants. It's a good mix of shopping, dining, and enjoying the atmosphere of Bratislava."

Aupark Shopping Center: A Local's Perspective

Aupark Shopping Center is one of Bratislava's largest and most popular malls, offering a diverse shopping experience, modern amenities, and an excellent location along the Dunaj River. Whether you're looking for the latest fashion trends, electronics, or simply a place to relax, Aupark has something for everyone.

Important Highlights:

- Wide Range of Shops: Aupark features a mix of international brands like Nike, Lacoste, and H&M, along with local Slovak stores. It caters to all tastes and budgets, making it ideal for both casual shoppers and those looking for high-end fashion.
- Dining Options: The food court is a highlight of Aupark, offering a variety of dining options. From quick snacks and coffee shops to sit-down restaurants serving Slovak and international cuisines, there's something to suit every craving.
- Entertainment: Beyond shopping, Aupark offers entertainment for all ages, including a cinema and various events. It's a great place to spend a day with family or friends.
- Riverside Views: Located along the Danube, the mall provides beautiful views of the river, with outdoor seating areas where you can enjoy a peaceful moment. The nearby promenade is perfect for a walk after your shopping.

How to Get There:

- Walking: Aupark is located about 15 minutes on foot from Bratislava Old Town. Simply head towards the Dunaj River and follow the path along the water.
- Tram: You can take tram line 1 or tram line 4 to the Aupark stop, which is right outside the mall. It's a quick and convenient option for getting there.

From Jana, a Local Resident:

"I visit Aupark at least once a week. It's a great place to do all my shopping in one place, and I love the selection of restaurants—there's always something new to try. The views of the river make it a lovely spot to unwind after a long shopping spree."

From Tomáš, a Local Resident:

"Aupark is perfect for when I need a quick shopping fix. The mall is huge and has a fantastic mix of shops. I like the cinema and enjoy grabbing a bite at the food court. It's also great that it's right by the river, making it a nice spot to relax after shopping."

Markets: Where to Find Authentic Souvenirs

Milan Rastislav Štefánik Market: A Local's Perspective

Milan Rastislav Štefánik Market (also known simply as Štefánikova Market) is one of the oldest and most traditional markets in Bratislava, offering a mix of fresh produce, local goods, and authentic Slovak flavors. Situated near the heart of the city, the market provides a unique experience for both locals and visitors who want to taste the essence of Bratislava's culinary culture.

Important Highlights:

- Fresh Produce: The market is known for its fresh fruits, vegetables, and local cheeses, making it a great spot for anyone looking for high-quality, locally sourced ingredients. You can find everything from fresh herbs to meats, often from nearby farms.
- Traditional Slovak Goods: In addition to fresh produce, the market also offers an array of traditional Slovak products, including handmade crafts, honey, and local wines. It's a perfect place to pick up unique souvenirs or gifts.
- Street Food: You'll often find street food stalls offering quick bites like lokše (traditional Slovak potato pancakes) or koláče (sweet pastries), providing a tasty introduction to Slovak flavors.
- Local Atmosphere: The market has a warm, bustling vibe with locals chatting with vendors, making it an authentic Slovak experience. It's a great way to interact with Bratislava's community and get a feel for local life.

How to Get There:

- Walking: The market is located around 10-15 minutes on foot from Bratislava Old Town. Walk towards Špitálska Street, and the market will be on your left, near Karadžičova Street.
- Tram: You can take tram line 4 or tram line 1 to the Karadžičova stop, which is only a few minutes' walk from the market.

From Lucia, a Local Resident:

"I love going to Štefánik Market early in the morning. It's the best place to grab fresh fruit and vegetables, and I can always find something unique. Plus, I can't resist the smell of lokše being made right there. It feels like a real slice of local life."

From Ján, a Local Resident:

"This market is where I do most of my shopping for fresh produce. It's not only about getting groceries but also enjoying the atmosphere. There's always something new, like fresh bread or homemade cheeses, and the people here are really friendly. It's a must-visit for anyone looking to experience Bratislava off the tourist path."

Tržnica Petržalka: A Local's Perspective

Tržnica Petržalka is a bustling, traditional market located in the Petržalka district of Bratislava. Known for its local flavor and variety of goods, it offers an authentic experience, especially for those looking to immerse themselves in Bratislava's everyday life. The market is a great place to shop for fresh produce, homemade products, and more, all at affordable prices.

Important Highlights:

- Fresh Produce and Local Goods: Tržnica Petržalka is famous for its fresh fruits, vegetables, meats, and dairy products. Local farmers and vendors come here to sell their high-quality produce, making it a great spot for those looking for fresh ingredients.
- Traditional Slovak Items: The market also features handcrafted products, such as local honey, handmade crafts, and freshly baked bread. It's the perfect place to pick up unique, traditional Slovak items.
- Street Food and Snacks: For a quick bite, you'll find food stalls offering traditional Slovak street food like klobása (sausage) and lokše (potato pancakes), giving you a taste of local flavors while you shop.
- Casual, Local Atmosphere: Unlike the more tourist-centric markets in the city, Tržnica Petržalka offers a very local, laid-back experience. It's a spot where you can interact with the community and get a feel for everyday Bratislava life.

How to Get There:

- Walking: From the Petržalka Train Station, the market is about a 5-minute walk. Simply head towards Karadžičova Street, and you'll find the market on the right.
- Tram: You can take tram line 4 to the Petržalka stop, which is right near the market entrance, making it easy to reach.

From Zuzana, a Local Resident:

"I visit Tržnica Petržalka for my weekly shopping. The produce is always fresh and affordable, and I love that I can find so many local products here. It feels like a real part of the neighborhood. Plus, grabbing a quick bite of klobása after shopping is always a treat!"

From Martin, a Local Resident:

"This market is one of my favorites in Bratislava. It's not as crowded as other markets, and you can always find great deals on fresh produce. The atmosphere is casual, and I love talking to the vendors. It's a great place to get local goods while avoiding the touristy spots."

Central Market (Centrálny Trh): A Local's Perspective

Central Market (Centrálny Trh) is one of the oldest and most iconic markets in Bratislava, located in the heart of the city. Known for its charming atmosphere and variety of fresh, local goods, it's a place where both locals and visitors can experience the city's food culture. From fresh produce to local delicacies, Centrálny Trh has something for everyone.

Important Highlights:

- Fresh Produce: The market is renowned for its selection of fresh fruits, vegetables, meats, and dairy products, many of which come directly from local Slovak farms. It's a perfect stop for anyone looking to buy high-quality, fresh ingredients.
- Slovak Specialties: Alongside the fresh produce, you'll find a variety of local Slovak products like honey, cheeses, and homemade bread. It's a great place to pick up authentic Slovak goods and try something new.
- Cafes and Street Food: The market has a number of street food stalls where you can enjoy traditional Slovak snacks, such as lokše (potato pancakes) or a hot klobása (sausage). It's also home to a few cafes where you can take a break and enjoy a coffee.
- Historic Charm: Located in a historic building, Centrálny Trh offers more than just a place to shop—it's an experience. The beautiful architecture adds to the charm, making it a favorite spot for both locals and tourists who appreciate the history of Bratislava.

How to Get There:

- Walking: Centrálny Trh is situated just a 5-minute walk from Bratislava Old Town. From Hlavné námestie (Main Square), head towards Mlynské Nivy Street, and you'll easily find the market.
- Tram: You can also take tram line 1 to the Karadžičova stop, and from there, it's a short walk to the market.

From Martina, a Local Resident:

"I love going to Centrálny Trh for my groceries. The produce here is always fresh, and I can always count on finding local specialties. I love buying Slovak cheese and bread and enjoying some lokše as a snack while I shop."

From Jozef, a Local Resident:

"Centrálny Trh is a perfect blend of history and local life. It's one of my favorite spots to buy fresh vegetables and meats. The atmosphere is lively, and the fact that it's located in such a historic building makes it even more special. I always make time to grab a coffee here."

Christmas Markets (During the Holiday Season): A Local's Perspective

The Christmas Markets in Bratislava are a magical experience, offering a warm and festive atmosphere that transforms the city into a winter wonderland. During the holiday season, the markets are filled with twinkling lights, traditional food, handcrafted goods, and the scents of mulled wine and roasted chestnuts. The markets are not only a place for shopping but also a perfect way to enjoy the holiday spirit with friends and family.

Important Highlights:

- Handmade Crafts and Souvenirs: The Christmas Markets are an excellent place to find handcrafted gifts, Christmas ornaments, and traditional Slovak souvenirs. Local artisans sell unique products, including wooden toys, ceramics, and handmade candles, perfect for gifts or keepsakes.
- Festive Food and Drinks: Traditional holiday treats such as lokše (potato pancakes), trdelník (sweet pastry), and roasted chestnuts are common sights at the market stalls. Don't miss out on a warm cup of mulled wine (called varené víno) to keep you cozy as you stroll through the market.
- Live Music and Performances: Many of the markets feature live Christmas carols, choirs, and folk performances, creating a lively atmosphere. Some markets even host small holiday concerts, adding to the festive spirit.
- Glistening Lights and Decorations: The market stalls are adorned with sparkling lights, and the streets around the market are beautifully decorated, creating a perfect holiday ambiance. The atmosphere is warm and festive, despite the cold winter weather.

How to Get There:

- Old Town Christmas Market: The main Christmas market is held in Hlavné námestie (Main Square) and stretches to Františkánske námestie (Franciscan Square). This market is centrally located and easily accessible by foot from almost anywhere in the Old Town.
- Other Locations: There are also smaller markets at Hviezdoslavovo námestie and Eurovea Mall along the Danube River.
- Tram: You can take tram lines 1 or 4 to Karadžičova or Františkánske námestie stops, depending on which market you want to visit.

From Ivana, a Local Resident:

"The Christmas markets in Bratislava are a yearly tradition for my family. We love to walk through the Old Town, soaking in the decorations, and grabbing a hot trdelník or mulled wine. It really feels like Christmas here, and the handmade crafts are perfect for picking up gifts."

From Peter, a Local Resident:

"I always look forward to the Christmas markets. The live music and holiday atmosphere really make it feel like a celebration. I usually grab some roasted chestnuts and enjoy the lights with friends. It's a wonderful way to enjoy the holiday season in Bratislava."

Chapter 10. Outdoor Adventures

Hiking in the Small Carpathians

Hiking in the Small Carpathians: A Local's Perspective

The Small Carpathians (Malé Karpaty) offer some of the best hiking opportunities just a short distance from Bratislava. This mountain range, which stretches north and east of the city, is an excellent escape for nature lovers and hikers, offering scenic views, picturesque trails, and a quiet retreat from the hustle and bustle of urban life. Whether you're an experienced hiker or a beginner, the Small Carpathians offer a variety of trails that are accessible year-round.

Important Highlights:

- Stunning Views: The Small Carpathians offer breathtaking views of the surrounding countryside, including rolling hills, deep forests, and small villages. On clear days, you can see all the way to the Danube River and the city of Bratislava.
- Variety of Trails: There are numerous hiking trails with varying levels of difficulty. Some popular ones include:
    - Záruby Hill: The highest peak in the range, offering a panoramic view of the area.
    - Pajštún Castle: A moderate hike that leads you to the ruins of a medieval castle, surrounded by forest paths.
    - Devin Castle Loop: A shorter, easier trail that takes you to the Devin Castle, with beautiful views of the confluence of the Morava and Danube Rivers.
- Wildlife and Nature: The Small Carpathians are rich in wildlife, and you may encounter deer, wild boar, and a variety of birds along the trails. The area is also home to diverse flora, including oak forests, beech trees, and wildflowers in the spring.
- Wine Culture: The region is also famous for its vineyards and wine-making traditions. After a hike, you can enjoy a glass of local wine in one of the many charming vineyards or small wineries scattered along the hills.

How to Get There:

- By Car: The Small Carpathians are easily accessible by car from Bratislava. You can drive to popular trailheads like Devin (where you can start the Devin Castle loop) or Pajštún Castle in about 20-30 minutes from the city center. There are free parking areas near most trailheads.
- Public Transport: You can take a bus or train from Bratislava to towns like Devin or Záhorská Bystrica, where many hiking trails begin. From there, it's a short walk to the trailheads. For example, a bus from Bratislava to Devin takes about 20 minutes.
- Guided Tours: For those who prefer a guided experience, several local companies offer guided hikes in the Small Carpathians, providing insights into the local flora, fauna, and history of the region.

Cost:

- Free Hiking: Most of the hiking trails in the Small Carpathians are free to access. There is no entry fee for hiking, and you can freely enjoy the natural beauty of the area.
- Guided Tours: If you prefer a guided hiking experience, prices usually range from €20 to €40 per person for a half-day tour, depending on the tour provider and the trail.
- Public Transport: A one-way bus ticket from Bratislava to Devin costs around €1.50 to €2.

From Veronika, a Local Resident:

"I love escaping to the Small Carpathians whenever I need a break. The trails are easy to access, and the views from Záruby Hill are incredible. It's a peaceful place to reconnect with nature, and I often stop by a local winery for some fresh wine after the hike."

From Milan, a Local Resident:

"Hiking in the Small Carpathians is always a great way to spend a weekend. I usually take the Devin Castle loop because it's relatively short but still offers stunning views of the river. It's also nice that the trails are free and so close to the city. It's a hidden gem for people in Bratislava!"

Cycling Along the Danube River: A Local's Perspective

Cycling along the Danube River in Bratislava offers one of the most scenic and accessible bike routes in Europe. Whether you're a seasoned cyclist or just looking for a leisurely ride, this stretch of the EuroVelo 6 bike trail provides incredible views of the river, the city, and the surrounding natural landscapes. It's an ideal way to explore the area at your own pace, while enjoying the fresh air and tranquility of the riverbanks.

Important Highlights:

- Scenic Views of the Danube: The Danube River offers stunning views as you cycle along its banks. On one side, you can admire the Bratislava Old Town with its historic buildings, while on the other side, you'll pass lush green areas, peaceful parks, and beautiful waterfront spots. The route is flat, making it suitable for cyclists of all skill levels.
- Connecting Key Landmarks: Along the way, you'll pass important Bratislava landmarks like the Bratislava Castle, the UFO Observation Deck (on the Nový Most bridge), and Eurovea Mall. You can stop at scenic spots to take pictures or enjoy a break.
- Bike-Friendly Infrastructure: The Danube bike path is well-marked and separated from pedestrian areas in most sections, ensuring a smooth and safe ride. The path runs alongside the river for about 40 kilometers within the city, but you can easily extend your ride into surrounding areas such as Petržalka or further out to Vienna (if you're up for a longer journey).
- Relaxed Stops and Cafes: There are plenty of opportunities to stop for a break, with cafes and beer gardens along the river. A popular spot is the Sad Janka Kráľa Park in Petržalka, which is right next to the trail, offering a peaceful environment to relax.
- Wildlife and Nature: Cycling along the river, you may also catch glimpses of local wildlife, including various birds and the occasional fish jumping in the river. The path runs through lush greenery, creating a sense of being immersed in nature while staying close to the city.

How to Get There:

- **By Bike:** If you're already in Bratislava, you can easily access the bike path from anywhere in the city center. The EuroVelo 6 trail is well-connected to the main city roads and can be accessed near Bratislava Castle or Eurovea Shopping Mall along the riverbank.
- **Bike Rental:** There are several bike rental shops near the city center or along the river, where you can rent a bike for the day. Most bike rental services will provide helmets and maps of the bike path.
    - Popular rental spots include City Bike Bratislava and Bikeshop Bratislava, where you can rent a bike for around €10-15 per day.
- **Public Transport:** If you don't want to ride all the way to the starting point, you can take your bike on public transport. Buses, trams, and trains in Bratislava allow bicycles for a small fee, which is usually around €1.

Cost:

- **Cycling:** There is no entry fee to cycle along the Danube River, as the bike path is open to the public.
- **Bike Rental:** If you don't have your own bike, renting one will cost around €10-15 per day, depending on the rental company and type of bike. E-bikes may be available for an additional fee.
- **Public Transport:** A single-ride public transport ticket with a bike is about €1.

From Kamil, a Local Resident:

"Cycling along the Danube is one of my favorite activities, especially during spring and summer. The views of the river and Bratislava Castle are breathtaking. It's also really relaxing to stop at a café by the river for a coffee or cold drink. It's an easy ride, even for beginners, and you can explore at your own pace."

From Ivana, a Local Resident:

"I love taking my bike along the river when I want a break from the city. The path is so peaceful, and the area around Eurovea Mall has great spots for a pit stop. Whether you're cycling for exercise or just for fun, it's the perfect way to enjoy Bratislava from a different perspective."

Chapter 11. Day Trips from Bratislava

The Small Carpathian Wine Region

Day Trip: The Small Carpathian Wine Region

The Small Carpathian Wine Region, just a short distance from Bratislava, is a hidden gem for wine lovers and nature enthusiasts alike. Located between the Small Carpathian mountain range and the plains of western Slovakia, this region offers more than just scenic vineyards. It's a place where history, tradition, and stunning landscapes come together, making it the perfect escape from the bustling city.

Highlights of the Small Carpathian Wine Region

1. The Vineyards and Wine Cellars

The area is home to some of Slovakia's finest wines, with vineyards stretching over gentle hills. As you wander through the vineyards, you'll see rows of grapes ripening under the sun, surrounded by the soft, rolling hills of the Carpathians. Many local wineries offer tours, where you can learn about the wine-making process, from grape harvest to fermentation. Tastings of local wines, including the well-known *Devín* and *Frankovka*, are a must. The rich flavors of the wines paired with the beautiful surroundings create an experience that feels both personal and authentic.

2. Cultural and Historic Sites

The region is steeped in history. Among the vineyards, you'll find charming villages like Pezinok and Modra, where locals still live the slow-paced life of the countryside. Modra is also known for its centuries-old pottery tradition, and you can visit the pottery workshops to see how this ancient craft is still practiced. In Pezinok, the *Museum of Wine* provides fascinating insight into the long-standing wine culture of the area.

3. Hiking and Scenic Views

For nature lovers, the Small Carpathians are perfect for hiking. Several well-marked trails lead through the vineyards and up to hilltops where you can enjoy panoramic views of the region. The area is especially beautiful in the autumn when the vines are covered in red and yellow leaves.

4. Wine Festivals and Events

Depending on the time of year, you might catch one of the local wine festivals or events that celebrate the harvest season. These festivals are a great way to sample a variety of wines, enjoy local food, and mingle with the locals who are eager to share their pride in their region.

How to Get There: A Local Perspective

Maria and Jozef's Experience

Maria and Jozef, both locals from Bratislava, have made countless trips to the Small Carpathian Wine Region. Here's their take on how to get there and what to expect:

Maria:
"We usually take the bus or a car to get there. The drive is beautiful, and it doesn't take long at all. We love going in the spring or fall when the weather is mild. From Bratislava, you can take a bus from the main bus station. It's about a 30-minute ride to Pezinok, and from there, it's easy to get to the vineyards. I recommend getting off in Pezinok and taking a short walk through the town—it's a lovely place to explore on foot."

Jozef:
"We also like driving. It gives us the freedom to stop wherever we want. The roads are quite straightforward, and within 30 minutes, we're right in the heart of the wine region. On weekends, we sometimes head to Modra first, where we grab some coffee and take a stroll around the village. The local cafes have the best pastries, especially if you're in the mood for something sweet with your coffee."

Maria:
"Once we're in the area, we always visit one of our favorite wineries. There's a place called *Vinárstvo Masaryk*, not far from Pezinok. It's run by a family, and their wines are some of the best in the region. We take a tour of the cellar, and after that, we sit down for a tasting. Jozef always enjoys their *Rizling*, and I prefer a glass of *Devín*. The views from the terrace are breathtaking, and you can see the vineyards stretching out for miles."

Jozef:
"After the wine tasting, we like to go for a short hike. The trail up to the *Karpaty* ridge is perfect for a light walk. It's not too difficult, and once you reach the top, you're rewarded with an incredible view of the surrounding vineyards and the city of Bratislava in the distance. We usually pack a small picnic, enjoy the view, and just relax for a bit."

Maria:
"If we're there on the right weekend, we sometimes catch a wine festival in Pezinok. It's always fun—there are lots of local vendors, live music, and, of course, plenty of wine to taste. It's not as touristy as other places, which is why we love it. You really get the sense of the region's traditions."

Jozef:
"If you're into history, a stop in Modra is a must. The pottery there is beautiful, and I've bought a few pieces for the house. We also like visiting the *Cerveny Kamen Castle* nearby. It's not too far from the vineyards, and it has a great history, plus the surrounding area is perfect for a peaceful walk."

Day Trip to Vienna (Austria)

Day Trip: Vienna, Austria

Vienna, the capital of Austria, is a city full of history, art, and culture, making it the perfect day trip from Bratislava. Just an hour away, Vienna offers everything from grand imperial palaces to world-class museums and beautiful parks. For Bratislava locals like Maria and Jozef, it's the ideal getaway when they want to experience something different, yet close to home.

Highlights of Vienna

1. Schönbrunn Palace

The magnificent Schönbrunn Palace, once the summer residence of the Habsburg monarchs, is a must-see. With its stunning gardens and elegant rooms, it's a window into the splendor of Austria's imperial past. You can tour the palace, walk through the vast gardens, and even visit the zoo, one of the oldest in the world.

2. St. Stephen's Cathedral (Stephansdom)

Located in the heart of Vienna, St. Stephen's Cathedral is a gothic masterpiece with stunning architecture. You can climb the tower for a panoramic view of the city or simply admire the intricate details of the building's design.

3. The Hofburg Palace

Another imperial landmark, the Hofburg Palace is the former residence of the Habsburgs and now houses several museums, the imperial chapel, and the Spanish Riding School. You can explore the museum and see the imperial treasures, or just enjoy the grandeur of the palace grounds.

4. The Belvedere Palace and Gardens

The Belvedere Palace is home to one of the world's most important art collections, including works by Klimt, Schiele, and other Austrian artists. The beautiful gardens surrounding the palace offer a peaceful retreat, with excellent views of the city.

5. Prater Park and the Giant Ferris Wheel

For a bit of fun, head to Prater Park, where you can take a ride on the famous Giant Ferris Wheel. This iconic attraction has been offering stunning views of the city since 1897 and is one of Vienna's most recognizable landmarks.

How to Get There: A Local Perspective

Maria and Jozef's Experience

Maria and Jozef, locals from Bratislava, often take the trip to Vienna for a day of sightseeing and exploration. Here's what they have to say about getting there and what to expect:

Maria:
"We love going to Vienna because it's so close to Bratislava, but it feels like a completely different world. We usually take the train because it's comfortable and gives us time to relax and enjoy the views. The train ride is about an hour, and it goes directly from the main train station in Bratislava to the Vienna city center. The trains run regularly, so it's easy to plan a spontaneous trip."

Jozef:
"I prefer the train, too. It's so easy. The ticket is cheap, and the service is great. You don't have to worry about traffic or parking in Vienna, which can be a hassle. We usually get off at *Wien Hauptbahnhof* (Vienna's main train station), which is right by the city center. From there, it's just a short ride on the metro to get to most of the main sights."

Maria:
"When we arrive, we usually head straight to *Stephansplatz* to see St. Stephen's Cathedral. The area around the cathedral is always lively with street performers, tourists, and locals. Afterward, we like to walk around the *Graben*, a beautiful pedestrian street full of shops, cafes, and restaurants. It's a nice place to stop for a coffee or snack before continuing our sightseeing."

Jozef:
"If we're feeling adventurous, we'll grab a tram to Schönbrunn Palace. We've been there so many times, but it never gets old. The palace gardens are especially beautiful in the spring and summer. We like to take our time exploring the gardens, but if we're in a rush, we'll just do a quick tour of the palace rooms. The interior is amazing, and it gives you a real sense of Austria's royal history."

Maria:
"After Schönbrunn, we usually head to the *Hofburg Palace* to see the imperial treasures. It's such a grand place, and there's so much to see. If you have time, you can visit the Spanish Riding School, too, to watch the famous Lipizzaner horses practice. It's a really unique experience."

Jozef:
"Another spot we love is *Prater Park*. If we're not too tired, we'll take a ride on the Ferris wheel. The view of Vienna from the top is spectacular, especially on a clear day. You can also get some traditional Austrian snacks there, like *würstl* (sausages) and *apfelstrudel* (apple strudel), which are always delicious."

Maria:
"If we're staying for lunch, we'll stop at a café in the city center. There's nothing quite like sitting at a traditional Viennese café, sipping coffee, and having a *Sachertorte* (chocolate cake). It's such an Austrian experience, and it's a great way to end our trip."

The Town of Trnava

Day Trip: The Town of Trnava

Located just about 45 kilometers from Bratislava, the town of Trnava is a charming and historic destination perfect for a day trip. Known as the "Slovak Rome" due to its numerous churches and religious sites, Trnava is a quiet town that offers a rich blend of history, culture, and local traditions. For Bratislava locals like Maria and Jozef, it's a great spot to explore, with a relaxed pace and a sense of history that feels a world away from the busy capital.

Highlights of Trnava

1. St. John the Baptist Cathedral (Trnava Cathedral)
   One of the most prominent landmarks in Trnava is the St. John the Baptist Cathedral. This stunning baroque-style cathedral is known for its impressive façade and beautiful interior. The cathedral's towering spires dominate the town's skyline, and its peaceful atmosphere makes it a wonderful place to visit.

2. City Walls and Towers
   Trnava is one of the few towns in Slovakia that still has remnants of its medieval city walls. You can walk along parts of these walls, which were originally built for protection in the 13th century. Several towers, including the City Tower and the St. Mikuláš Tower, offer great views over the town and its surroundings.

3. The Holy Trinity Column
   The Holy Trinity Column, located in the town square, is an iconic Baroque monument. It was built in the 18th century and features intricate sculptures and carvings. It's a key historical site in the center of the town and a beautiful example of Baroque architecture.

4. The Town Center and Main Square
   Trnava's main square is a lively area full of cafés, restaurants, and shops. The square is lined with colorful buildings, and you'll often find locals enjoying a coffee or chatting on the benches. It's a great place to take in the town's atmosphere and enjoy a leisurely afternoon.

5. Trnava University and the Library
   Trnava is home to one of Slovakia's oldest universities, Trnava University, founded in 1635. The university campus, with its historic buildings and peaceful courtyards, is worth a visit. The nearby library, housed in a beautiful baroque building, is also an interesting stop for those who enjoy architecture and history.

How to Get There: A Local Perspective

Maria and Jozef's Experience

Maria and Jozef, both from Bratislava, often make the short journey to Trnava to escape the bustle of the city and experience the more relaxed pace of life in this charming town. Here's what they have to say about how to get there and what they enjoy once they arrive:

Maria:
"Trnava is such a pleasant town, and it's only about 40 minutes by car from Bratislava. If we're driving, it's a really easy and straightforward route. We usually take the *D1* motorway, and there's plenty of parking available near the town center. Sometimes, if we feel like being more eco-friendly, we take the bus, which is also convenient. The buses from Bratislava leave from the main bus station and drop you off at the central bus station in Trnava, which is just a short walk to the town center."

Jozef:
"Taking the train is another good option. The train ride takes around 40 minutes, and it's a relaxing

journey. We get off at the main train station in Trnava, which is a short walk to the town square. The train station is easy to navigate, and once you're there, everything is close by."

Maria:
"Once we arrive in Trnava, we always start with a walk through the town center. We like to stop by the *Town Hall* and take a stroll through the square. The main square has this wonderful, peaceful atmosphere, and we always find a café where we can sit and enjoy a coffee. There's something about the slower pace here that makes it perfect for a relaxed day out."

Jozef:
"We usually walk to the *St. John the Baptist Cathedral* next. The cathedral is so impressive, and it's nice and quiet inside. We've been there a few times, but it never gets old. I especially enjoy the view from the top of the church tower. From there, you can see the entire town and the countryside around it."

Maria:
"Afterward, we head to the *City Walls* and *St. Mikuláš Tower*. Trnava's old city walls are such an interesting part of the town's history. They're not as famous as other fortifications in Slovakia, but we love the fact that they're still standing and you can walk along them. It gives you a great perspective of the town, especially if you climb up one of the towers. The view from the *St. Mikuláš Tower* is fantastic, and you can really appreciate the layout of the town from up there."

Jozef:
"For lunch, we usually grab something local at one of the small restaurants or pubs near the square. There are some great places to try Slovak dishes, like *lokše* (potato pancakes) or *zemiakové placky* (potato fritters). Afterward, we often walk to *Trnava University*. The campus is beautiful, with old buildings and gardens. The library there is one of the most impressive in the town, and sometimes we'll stop by just to admire the architecture."

Maria:
"If we're in the mood for a little more sightseeing, we'll visit the *Holy Trinity Column*. It's a beautiful Baroque monument, and it's hard to miss when you're in the main square. I love the intricate details on it, and it makes for a perfect photo opportunity."

Jozef:
"If the weather is nice, we'll end our day with a walk around *Trnava's Parks* or along the *Trnavka River*. The parks are peaceful and a great place to relax and unwind before heading back home. We always feel refreshed after a trip to Trnava."

The Hungarian Border: A Quick Trip to Komárno

Day Trip: The Hungarian Border – A Quick Trip to Komárno

Just a short journey south of Bratislava lies the town of Komárno, located right on the Hungarian border. This small Slovak town offers a unique blend of history, culture, and a distinct mix of Slovak and Hungarian influences. For Bratislava locals like Maria and Jozef, a visit to Komárno is a simple yet fascinating trip that allows them to explore both the natural beauty and the cultural fusion of two neighboring countries. Whether it's crossing the border, exploring ancient fortifications, or enjoying local food, Komárno makes for a delightful and easy day trip.

Highlights of Komárno

1. Komárno Fortress (Komárňanská pevnosť)
   Komárno is perhaps most famous for its massive fortress, which dates back to the 16th century. The Komárno Fortress complex is a series of well-preserved military structures, including bastions, ramparts, and tunnels. It offers visitors the chance to step back in time and learn about the town's strategic importance during various periods in history, especially its role in defending the Austro-Hungarian Empire. A walk around the fortress is like stepping into another era, with expansive views of the surrounding landscape and the Danube River.

2. The Bridge of Friendship
   One of the unique features of Komárno is the *Bridge of Friendship*, which connects Slovakia to Hungary. The bridge, which spans the Danube River, is an iconic symbol of the close relationship between the two countries. You can walk across it to step into Hungary, experiencing the change of atmosphere from Slovakia to Hungary in just a few minutes. It's a unique experience to visit two countries in one trip without having to go far.

3. The City Center and Town Square
   Komárno's town center has a beautiful, peaceful atmosphere with quaint streets and charming buildings. The main square is lined with cafes, small shops, and colorful buildings, making it a great place to relax and soak in the local culture. The square is also home to the Statue of the Holy Trinity, a Baroque monument that reflects the town's religious heritage. It's a lovely spot to take photos or enjoy a traditional Slovak coffee.

4. The Hungarian Cultural Center
   Given its proximity to Hungary, Komárno boasts a significant Hungarian influence, and the Hungarian Cultural Center is an excellent place to explore this aspect of the town. The center often hosts events, exhibitions, and performances that celebrate Hungarian traditions and art. It's a great stop for visitors looking to learn more about the Hungarian side of Komárno and the town's shared cultural history.

5. Danube River and Promenade
   The Danube River flows right through Komárno, and the riverside promenade offers a peaceful walk with beautiful views. The area is perfect for a leisurely stroll, and during the warmer months, you can relax by the water, watching boats pass by and enjoying the serenity of the river. There are also several cafes along the promenade where you can enjoy a drink with a view.

How to Get There: A Local Perspective

Maria and Jozef's Experience

Maria and Jozef, both Bratislava locals, enjoy visiting Komárno whenever they want to explore a new place that's just a short drive away. Here's how they make the most of their trips to this charming border town:

Maria:
"Komárno is just about an hour's drive from Bratislava, and it's one of those places where you don't have to rush. We usually take the *D2* highway south, which is a pretty straight route and not too crowded. We love how easy it is to get there—whether we're driving or catching the bus, it's a short journey, and there's no hassle."

Jozef:
"I prefer driving, too. The road is quite easy, and we often pass by vineyards and small villages on the way. It's a nice drive, especially when the weather is good. We always park in the center of Komárno, close to the fortress and the river. There's plenty of parking around, so we don't have to worry about finding a spot."

Maria:
"Once we get to Komárno, we always start by visiting the *Komárno Fortress*. The fortifications are so impressive, and we like to walk around the outer walls first. If we're in the mood for a deeper dive into the history, we go inside the museum where we can learn more about the fortress's military past. We especially like the panoramic views from the top of the walls. You can see the entire town and the Danube River winding through the landscape."

Jozef:
"After the fortress, we take a walk to the *Bridge of Friendship*. It's such a simple yet meaningful experience to walk from Slovakia into Hungary. The view of the Danube from the bridge is beautiful, and there's something special about standing in two countries at once. We like to take our time on the bridge, looking at the water and the surrounding area."

Maria:
"If we're feeling hungry, we usually head to the town square. There are a few good places to grab a bite—sometimes we get a coffee at one of the cafés, or we stop for lunch at a traditional Slovak restaurant. *Trdelník* (a sweet pastry) is always a good choice if we're in the mood for a snack!"

Jozef:
"We don't always stop at the Hungarian Cultural Center, but it's definitely worth visiting if you're interested in learning more about the Hungarian influence on the town. The center usually has interesting exhibits, and sometimes they host performances or cultural events. It's a good way to connect with the Hungarian side of Komárno."

Maria:
"If the weather is nice, we love walking along the Danube promenade. The area by the river is peaceful, and you can just sit and relax while enjoying the view of the water. We sometimes bring a picnic if we want to spend more time outdoors."

Chapter 12. Practical Travel Tips

Safety and Health Information

Safety and Health Information for Travelers in Bratislava

When visiting Bratislava or any new destination, ensuring your safety and well-being is essential for a smooth and enjoyable trip. While Slovakia is generally a safe and welcoming country for travelers, there are a few things to consider and be aware of to ensure your health and safety during your visit. Below are some important tips and practical advice related to safety and health in Bratislava.

---

1. General Safety in Bratislava

Bratislava is known for being a relatively safe city. Crime rates are low, and violent crime is rare. However, like in any major city, it's still wise to exercise common sense and take basic precautions:

- Pickpocketing: Although Bratislava is not known for widespread pickpocketing, it can occur in busy tourist spots, especially in crowded areas like the Old Town or public transportation hubs. Always keep an eye on your belongings, especially in crowded areas or on public transport.
    - Tip: Use anti-theft backpacks or money belts, and keep wallets, phones, and valuables securely stored in inner pockets or bags.
- Night Safety: Bratislava is generally safe at night, especially in the city center, where most bars and restaurants are located. However, it's recommended to avoid poorly lit and less trafficked areas late at night, especially when walking alone.
    - Tip: Always use well-lit and busy streets when walking after dark, and try to avoid secluded areas.
- Taxis and Ridesharing: When taking a taxi, it's advisable to use reputable services or apps like Bolt or Uber. Some taxi drivers may overcharge tourists, so it's best to ask for an estimated price or request the meter to be used. Using ridesharing apps ensures fair pricing and reliable service.
    - Tip: If using a taxi, make sure it's from an official company or ordered through a trusted app to avoid scams.

---

2. Health Information and Medical Care

While Slovakia has a high standard of healthcare, it's essential to understand what to do in case you need medical attention during your trip.

- Emergency Services: In case of an emergency, dial *112* for general emergency services or *155* for an ambulance. English-speaking operators are usually available, especially in larger cities like Bratislava.
- Hospitals and Clinics: Bratislava has several hospitals and clinics that offer quality medical care. Some major hospitals include:

- University Hospital Bratislava – One of the largest hospitals in the city, with emergency services available.
    - Poliklinika na Karadžičovej – A well-known polyclinic with general medical services.
- Most of these facilities have English-speaking staff, especially in emergency and urgent care departments.

- Pharmacies: Pharmacies are easily accessible in Bratislava, and most of them have English-speaking staff. Over-the-counter medications such as painkillers, cold medicine, and basic health products are readily available.
    - Tip: If you need specific prescription medication, check if it's available at pharmacies before your trip. Bring any necessary medical prescriptions in case you need to visit a local pharmacy.
- Health Insurance: It's essential to have travel insurance that includes coverage for medical expenses. If you're an EU citizen, your European Health Insurance Card (EHIC) will cover most medical services in Slovakia. Non-EU citizens should ensure they have adequate travel insurance that includes emergency medical care.

---

3. Health Precautions

Maintaining your health while traveling in Bratislava involves being prepared for local conditions and potential health risks. Here are some key health-related tips:

- Water Safety: Tap water in Bratislava is safe to drink, and it's regularly tested to meet EU standards. You can drink the water from fountains and in restaurants without worrying about contamination.
    - Tip: If you prefer bottled water, it's available in most supermarkets and restaurants.
- Food Safety: Slovak food is delicious and diverse, but it's always a good idea to exercise caution when trying street food or eating in unfamiliar places.
    - Tip: Always choose clean, reputable establishments for meals, and avoid food that looks like it has been left out for too long, especially in hot weather.
- Allergies: If you suffer from allergies, it's a good idea to check the pollen count before traveling, particularly during the spring months when pollen levels are high. In some areas of the city, air pollution can also be a concern, especially for those with respiratory conditions like asthma.
    - Tip: Bring necessary allergy medications with you, and check local air quality reports if you have respiratory concerns.

---

4. Transportation and Safety

Bratislava has an efficient and well-connected public transportation system, including buses, trams, and trolleybuses, which are reliable and affordable. However, like any city, there are a few things to keep in mind:

- Public Transport Safety: The public transport system in Bratislava is generally safe, but be cautious of pickpockets, especially in busy areas. Trams and buses can get crowded, and it's best to keep your belongings close.
  - Tip: Always have a valid ticket before entering public transportation. The *DPMB* (Bratislava Public Transport Company) offers tickets that can be purchased via vending machines, mobile apps, or from kiosks.
- Cycling: Bratislava has become more bike-friendly, with dedicated bike lanes and bike-sharing services such as *Slovenská cyklodoprava*. Cycling is a great way to explore the city, but be cautious on busy roads, and always wear a helmet.
  - Tip: If you're not familiar with cycling in urban areas, consider renting an e-scooter or using public transport instead.

---

5. Natural Hazards and Weather

Bratislava experiences four distinct seasons: mild springs, hot summers, crisp autumns, and cold winters. While it's generally a safe place weather-wise, here are a few things to consider:

- Summer Heat: Summer temperatures in Bratislava can climb to 30°C (86°F) or higher, which can be intense if you're not used to the heat.
  - Tip: Drink plenty of water, wear sunscreen, and take breaks in the shade to avoid heat exhaustion. A hat and sunglasses can also help protect you from the sun.
- Winter Cold: Winters in Bratislava can be cold, with temperatures often dropping below freezing. Snow is not uncommon, especially in December and January, so be cautious of icy sidewalks.
  - Tip: Wear warm clothing, including gloves, hats, and layers. Be especially careful on icy sidewalks to prevent slipping.
- Flooding: Bratislava is located along the Danube River, which can sometimes cause flooding in areas near the riverbank, especially during heavy rainfall. While major flooding is rare, it's something to be aware of.
  - Tip: Stay informed about the weather forecast and local alerts, especially during the spring and early summer months when rainfall is more likely.

Chapter 13. Suggested Itineraries

2-Day Itinerary: Exploring the Heart of the City

2-Day Itinerary: Exploring the Heart of Bratislava

Bratislava, the charming capital of Slovakia, is a city of contrasts. It combines medieval old-world charm with modern urban culture, set against the stunning backdrop of the Danube River and the Carpathian Mountains. In this 2-day itinerary, you'll explore the heart of the city, with a mix of historical landmarks, cultural gems, scenic walks, and delicious food. Get ready to immerse yourself in everything that makes Bratislava a unique and unforgettable destination.

Day 1: A Journey Through History and Architecture

Morning: Discovering the Old Town

9:00 AM - Breakfast at Café Mayer. Start your day at one of the city's most iconic cafes. Café Mayer, established in 1873, is known for its rich coffee and delicious pastries. The atmosphere here is a perfect blend of old-world charm and modern elegance, making it the ideal place to kick off your Bratislava adventure. Try a traditional Slovak pastry, such as *koláče*, paired with a strong coffee to fuel your day.

10:00 AM - Bratislava Castle: After breakfast, head to Bratislava Castle, perched atop a hill overlooking the city and the Danube River. This castle, dating back to the 9th century, offers not only a fascinating history but also breathtaking panoramic views of the city and beyond. Explore the castle grounds, visit the Slovak National Museum housed within, and admire the impressive gardens. The castle's mix of Baroque and Gothic architecture is a sight to behold.

- Tip: Arrive early to avoid the crowds and take your time walking around the castle's expansive grounds.

11:30 AM - St. Martin's Cathedral: Just a short walk down from the castle is St. Martin's Cathedral, one of the oldest and most important churches in Bratislava. The cathedral is known for its impressive Gothic architecture and its historical significance—it was once the coronation site of Hungarian kings. Take a moment to admire the interior and its stunning stained-glass windows.

Afternoon: Exploring the Old Town

1:00 PM - Lunch at Modrá Hviezda: For lunch, head to Modrá Hviezda, a traditional Slovak restaurant located in the Old Town. This charming spot offers classic Slovak dishes in a cozy, rustic atmosphere. Try *bryndzové halušky* (potato dumplings with sheep cheese) or *goulash* served with fresh bread. It's the perfect place to taste the local flavors.

2:30 PM - Old Town Square and Michael's Gate: After lunch, take a leisurely walk through the Old Town Square, where you can admire the vibrant architecture of Bratislava's medieval buildings. Be sure to visit

Michael's Gate, the only remaining city gate from the medieval fortifications, offering a glimpse into the city's past.

3:30 PM - Walk along the Danube Promenade: For a relaxing afternoon, head to the Danube Promenade. This scenic area along the river offers picturesque views of the Danube, with paths for walking or cycling. You can sit on a bench, enjoy the view, or grab a refreshing drink at one of the riverside cafés.

- Optional: If you're feeling adventurous, take a boat cruise along the Danube to get a different perspective of the city.

Evening: Slovak Culture and Dining

6:00 PM - Visit the Slovak National Theatre or a Museum: If you enjoy culture, catch a performance at the Slovak National Theatre, one of the oldest and most esteemed theatres in the country. Alternatively, you can visit the Slovak National Gallery or the Primate's Palace, known for its grand halls and historical significance.

8:00 PM - Dinner at Hradná reštaurácia: End your day with dinner at Hradná reštaurácia, a charming restaurant located near Bratislava Castle, offering traditional Slovak food in a medieval-style setting. The restaurant serves a variety of dishes such as roasted duck, venison, and hearty stews. Pair your meal with a glass of local wine or a traditional Slovak beer.

Day 2: Contemporary Bratislava and Hidden Gems

Morning: Modern Art and Architecture

9:00 AM - Breakfast at Urban House: Start your second day with a modern twist. Head to Urban House, a trendy café located in the Old Town, known for its relaxed atmosphere and delicious breakfast options. You can enjoy a fresh smoothie bowl, avocado toast, or a classic egg and bacon breakfast to fuel up for your day of exploring.

10:00 AM - The Blue Church (St. Elizabeth's Church): After breakfast, make your way to one of the most unique landmarks in the city—the Blue Church (St. Elizabeth's Church). This stunning church, built in the early 20th century, is famous for its vibrant blue color and Art Nouveau design. Its delicate and intricate design makes it one of Bratislava's hidden gems.

11:00 AM - The Grassalkovich Palace (Presidential Palace): Next, head to the Grassalkovich Palace, the official residence of the President of Slovakia. While you cannot enter the palace, you can take a stroll through its beautiful palace gardens, which are open to the public. This spot offers a peaceful escape from the busy city and provides a beautiful setting for a relaxing walk.

Afternoon: Shopping and Hidden Gems

12:30 PM - Lunch at Bratislava Flagship Market: Head over to Bratislava Flagship Market (located near the Old Town) for a casual yet delicious lunch. This modern food market features local and international vendors selling everything from gourmet burgers to fresh pastries and traditional Slovak dishes. It's a great spot to sample a variety of flavors and enjoy the lively atmosphere.

2:00 PM - Visit the Slovak Radio Building (The "Upside Down Pyramid"): For architecture enthusiasts, a visit to the Slovak Radio Building is a must. This striking building, with its upside-down pyramid design, is one of the most famous examples of modernist architecture in Bratislava. While not typically open to the public, it's worth admiring from the outside and learning about its unique design.

3:00 PM - Petržalka District and the New Bridge: To explore the more modern side of Bratislava, head across the New Bridge (most famous for its UFO-shaped observation deck) to the Petržalka district. This area is home to large Soviet-era apartment blocks but also has several modern spots to explore, including a few quirky cafes and local boutiques.

- Optional: Take the elevator to the UFO Observation Deck for panoramic views of the city, the Danube River, and the surrounding countryside.

Evening: Relax and Unwind

5:00 PM - Visit the Old Town for Souvenir Shopping: Return to the Old Town for some last-minute souvenir shopping. You'll find a variety of shops selling handmade goods, local pottery, and traditional Slovak souvenirs like wooden toys, crystal, and lace.

7:00 PM - Dinner at Slovenská Reštaurácia: For your final dinner in Bratislava, indulge in Slovak cuisine at Slovenská Reštaurácia, where you can enjoy traditional dishes like *kapustnica* (sauerkraut soup), *lokše* (potato pancakes), or a *rožky* bread dish. Pair it with a local wine or *Slovenský Kvas*, a fermented beverage popular in Slovakia.

8:30 PM - Evening Walk Around the Old Town: Finish your trip with a peaceful evening walk through the Old Town, where the charming streets are beautifully lit up at night. The square near the Main Square and Old Town Hall is a lovely spot to reflect on your trip. If you're in the mood, stop by a cozy bar to enjoy a cocktail or local drink before saying goodbye to this beautiful city.

4-Day Itinerary: A Deeper Dive into Bratislava

4-Day Itinerary: A Deeper Dive into Bratislava

Bratislava is a city rich in history, culture, and modern charm. With four days to explore, you can truly immerse yourself in the beauty and diversity of the Slovak capital. From exploring the historical Old Town to discovering modern art and culture, this itinerary will guide you through the heart of Bratislava, offering a well-rounded experience of the city's finest attractions and hidden gems.

Day 1: Exploring the Heart of Old Town

Morning: Immerse Yourself in Bratislava's History

9:00 AM – Breakfast at Café Mayer: Start your adventure with a traditional Slovak breakfast at Café Mayer, one of the oldest and most elegant coffee houses in the city. Enjoy a coffee paired with pastries such as *koláče* (traditional Slovak pastries) and perhaps a local breakfast favorite like *trdelník* (a sweet pastry cooked over an open flame).

10:00 AM – Bratislava Castle: After breakfast, make your way to Bratislava Castle, a symbol of Slovak history. Perched on a hill overlooking the city, the castle offers fantastic views of the Danube River and the surrounding landscape. Wander through its various courtyards and gardens, and take time to visit the Slovak National Museum inside the castle, which covers Slovakia's rich history, from prehistoric times to the present.

12:00 PM – St. Martin's Cathedral: Just a short walk from the castle, you'll find St. Martin's Cathedral, a striking Gothic building that was once the coronation church of Hungarian kings. Take a moment to appreciate the beautiful architecture, the serene interior, and the historical significance of the site.

Afternoon: Discover Old Town Charm

1:00 PM – Lunch at Modrá Hviezda: For lunch, head to Modrá Hviezda, a cozy, traditional Slovak restaurant located in the heart of the Old Town. Try classic Slovak dishes such as *bryndzové halušky* (potato dumplings with sheep cheese) or *kapustnica* (sauerkraut soup).

2:30 PM – Old Town Exploration: After lunch, take a leisurely walk around Bratislava's Old Town, with its cobbled streets, charming squares, and colorful facades. Make sure to visit Michael's Gate, one of the last remaining medieval gates of the city. Nearby, you'll find Primate's Palace, a beautiful palace with a stunning hall that once hosted significant political events.

4:00 PM – Walk Along the Danube Promenade: After exploring the Old Town, head down to the Danube Promenade for a relaxing stroll along the river. This scenic walk offers fantastic views of the river, and you can sit on a bench and enjoy the peaceful atmosphere or visit one of the riverside cafés for a refreshing drink.

Evening: Dinner and Relaxation

6:30 PM – Dinner at Hradná Reštaurácia: End your day with a traditional Slovak dinner at Hradná Reštaurácia, a cozy restaurant near the Bratislava Castle. Enjoy classic Slovak dishes like roasted duck or venison, paired with local wine or a traditional Slovak beer.

8:00 PM – Evening Walk in the Old Town: After dinner, take a peaceful evening stroll through the Old Town, where the charming streets are beautifully lit at night. Stop by Main Square to admire the Old Town Hall, a perfect spot for some evening photos.

Day 2: Art, Culture, and Modern Bratislava

Morning: Dive into Modern Art

9:00 AM – Breakfast at Urban House: Start the day with breakfast at Urban House, a trendy café in the city center. It offers a relaxed atmosphere and great breakfast options like smoothie bowls, avocado toast, or classic eggs and bacon.

10:00 AM – The Slovak National Gallery: Spend your morning at the Slovak National Gallery, home to an impressive collection of Slovak and international art. The gallery is housed in a beautiful Baroque building, and its exhibits span from classical works to contemporary art. Don't miss the gallery's collection of works by Slovak painters and sculptors.

11:30 AM – The Blue Church (St. Elizabeth's Church): Next, head to St. Elizabeth's Church, also known as the Blue Church. This stunning building is famous for its vibrant blue color and unique Art Nouveau design. Take a moment to admire the architecture and the intricate details inside.

Afternoon: Modern Bratislava and Hidden Gems

1:00 PM – Lunch at Bratislava Flagship Market: For lunch, head to the Bratislava Flagship Market, an indoor food market offering local and international cuisine. Enjoy freshly prepared street food, local Slovak specialties, or international bites from food stalls. It's a great spot to try something new and experience Bratislava's contemporary food scene.

2:00 PM – Visit the Slovak Radio Building (UFO Tower): After lunch, make your way to the Slovak Radio Building, an iconic modernist structure shaped like an upside-down pyramid. You can't enter the building itself, but the UFO Tower nearby offers one of the best views of the city. Take the elevator to the observation deck for panoramic views of Bratislava and the Danube River.

3:30 PM – Petržalka District: Take a walk across the New Bridge to explore the Petržalka district, known for its large Soviet-era apartment blocks. While the area might seem stark and utilitarian, it's a great place to get a glimpse of Bratislava's post-communist urban growth. Take a moment to explore its modern cafes, art galleries, and parks.

Evening: Explore Bratislava's Nightlife

6:30 PM – Dinner at Slovenská Reštaurácia: For dinner, enjoy traditional Slovak cuisine at Slovenská Reštaurácia. Located in the Old Town, it offers classic dishes such as *rožky* (Slovak bread dumplings) and *lokše* (potato pancakes), along with excellent local wine.

8:00 PM – Night Out in the Old Town: Finish the night by exploring the nightlife in Bratislava's Old Town. From lively pubs and craft beer bars to chic wine lounges, there are plenty of places to enjoy a drink. The Beer Palace offers a great selection of Slovak craft beers, while The Apartment is a cozy bar perfect for cocktails.

Day 3: Day Trips Around Bratislava

Morning: Day Trip to Devín Castle: 9:00 AM – Breakfast at Café Erste
Start the day with breakfast at Café Erste, located in the city center. Known for its delicious pastries and rich coffee, it's the perfect place to begin your day trip to Devín Castle.

10:00 AM – Visit Devín Castle: Take a short bus or taxi ride to Devín Castle, located about 15 minutes outside of the city center. The castle, sitting at the confluence of the Danube and Morava rivers, offers incredible views of the surrounding landscape and has an intriguing history. Explore the ruins, visit the museum, and learn about the castle's role in Slovakia's past.

Afternoon: A Taste of Wine in the Small Carpathian Wine Region

1:00 PM – Lunch at a Vineyard: After exploring Devín Castle, head to the Small Carpathian Wine Region, which is famous for its vineyards and wine culture. Visit a local winery for a traditional Slovak lunch paired with regional wines. Many vineyards offer guided tours where you can learn about Slovak wine production and taste some of the best local wines.

3:30 PM – Explore Local Vineyards: After lunch, take a leisurely walk through the vineyards of the Small Carpathians. The picturesque landscapes, with hills covered in vines, are a perfect backdrop for a relaxing afternoon. If you're a wine enthusiast, consider booking a wine-tasting tour to deepen your understanding of Slovakia's wine culture.

Evening: Return to Bratislava

6:00 PM – Return to Bratislava: Head back to Bratislava and unwind at your accommodation.

8:00 PM – Dinner at the Zlata Noha: Finish your day with a delicious dinner at Zlata Noha (Golden Paw), a cozy restaurant offering Slovak and Central European cuisine. Enjoy a hearty dish of *sviečková* (beef in creamy sauce) or *klobása* (local sausage), paired with a glass of Slovak wine.

Day 4: Leisure Day and Local Culture

Morning: Bratislava's Parks and Nature

9:00 AM – Breakfast at the Café in the Park: On your final day, enjoy breakfast in the relaxing environment of Železná studienka, a popular park in Bratislava. You'll find several cozy cafes in the park, perfect for starting the day in a tranquil setting surrounded by nature.

10:00 AM – Petržalka's Sad Janka Kráľa Park: Take a short walk to Sad Janka Kráľa, the oldest public park in Central Europe, located in the Petržalka district. Stroll through the park's manicured paths, enjoy the green spaces, and admire the surrounding views of the city and the river.

Afternoon: Visit Museums and Relax

12:00 PM – Visit the Museum of City History: For a deeper dive into the city's past, visit the Museum of City History located in the Old Town. The museum is housed in the Old Town Hall and offers exhibits about the history of Bratislava, from medieval times to the present.

2:00 PM – Relax at the Ondrejský Park: Take a leisurely walk through Ondrejský Park, one of Bratislava's peaceful green spaces. It's the perfect spot to relax and reflect on your trip before heading out for some final shopping or sightseeing.

Evening: Farewell Dinner in Bratislava

6:30 PM – Dinner at Savoy Restaurant: For your last evening, indulge in a fine dining experience at Savoy Restaurant, located inside the historic Hotel Carlton. Enjoy expertly prepared dishes with a mix of local and international flavors, paired with a fine selection of Slovak wines.

8:00 PM – Nighttime Views of the City: Finish your 4-day journey with a nighttime visit to the UFO Observation Deck for breathtaking views of Bratislava illuminated at night. It's the perfect way to say goodbye to the city, with one last stunning vista of the Danube River and the city lights below.

Family-Friendly Itinerary: Activities for All Ages

Family-Friendly Itinerary: Activities for All Ages in Bratislava

Bratislava is a wonderful destination for families, offering a perfect blend of history, culture, outdoor fun, and interactive activities for all ages. Whether you're traveling with young children, teenagers, or grandparents, there's something in the Slovak capital to keep everyone entertained. In this comprehensive itinerary, we'll guide you through family-friendly activities that are fun, educational, and provide plenty of opportunities for quality time together.

Day 1: Exploring History and Outdoor Fun

Morning: Start with History at Bratislava Castle

9:00 AM – Breakfast at Café Mayer: Begin your family adventure at Café Mayer, a charming café known for its pastries, sandwiches, and coffee. The warm and welcoming atmosphere is perfect for a relaxed family breakfast before heading out for the day.

10:00 AM – Bratislava Castle: Kick off your exploration with a visit to Bratislava Castle. This iconic site is both fun and educational for kids and adults alike. Kids will enjoy exploring the castle's expansive grounds, while adults can appreciate its historical significance and views of the city and Danube River.

- Tip: There are plenty of wide open spaces, so bring a picnic or a ball for the kids to play in the castle's gardens.
- Family-friendly activity: The Slovak National Museum located inside the castle offers exhibits that will fascinate children, including displays about the region's history and interactive exhibits.

11:30 AM – St. Martin's Cathedral: Walk down from the castle to St. Martin's Cathedral, which is a short walk away. The cathedral is historically significant as the site of royal coronations. It's a peaceful stop where the whole family can admire the Gothic architecture and explore the inside of one of Bratislava's oldest landmarks.

Afternoon: Fun and Learning in the Old Town

1:00 PM – Lunch at Modrá Hviezda: Head to Modrá Hviezda, a family-friendly restaurant in the Old Town. The restaurant offers delicious Slovak cuisine with a cozy and relaxed atmosphere, perfect for families. You can try traditional dishes like *halušky* (dumplings with sheep cheese) and *goulash* while the kids enjoy lighter options like soups or sandwiches.

2:30 PM – Interactive Fun at the City Museum: After lunch, walk over to the City Museum (housed in the Old Town Hall). The museum is engaging for both kids and adults, with exhibits about the city's history, medieval life, and the architecture of the Old Town. The interactive elements, such as the exhibits related to medieval Bratislava, will capture children's attention while learning about the city's past.

4:00 PM – Old Town Exploration: Take a stroll around Bratislava's Old Town, where cobbled streets and colorful buildings are waiting to be explored. Families can stop at some of the quirky shops or explore the famous Michael's Gate, the only remaining medieval gate in the city. Kids will love walking through it and imagining what the city was like centuries ago.

- Fun for Kids: Look for the Statue of Napoleon's Soldier on the streets of the Old Town. It's a great photo op for the family.

Evening: Relaxing Dinner and Playtime

6:00 PM – Dinner at the Zlata Noha: After a day of exploration, have dinner at Zlata Noha, a family-friendly restaurant offering Slovak and Central European cuisine. The restaurant is known for its warm atmosphere and delicious dishes, making it an excellent place for families to relax after a busy day of sightseeing.

8:00 PM – Evening Walk and Play in the Park: Finish the evening with a peaceful family walk through Sad Janka Kráľa Park, located in the Petržalka district. This park is one of the oldest public parks in Europe and is perfect for children to run around and play. It's a great place to unwind while the kids enjoy the open space.

Day 2: Nature, Animals, and Interactive Activities

Morning: Nature and Animal Fun

9:00 AM – Breakfast at Urban House: Start your day at Urban House, a family-friendly café offering a variety of breakfast options, from pancakes and eggs to healthy smoothie bowls. It's a great spot to fuel up for a day filled with outdoor adventures.

10:00 AM – Visit the Bratislava Zoo and Petržalka: Next, head to the Bratislava Zoo, located just a short drive from the city center. The zoo is home to a wide variety of animals, including lions, giraffes, and elephants. It's a fun and educational visit for kids of all ages. There's also a Children's Zoo where kids can interact with farm animals like goats and sheep. Be sure to stop by the zoo's play areas for some extra fun.

- Family Tip: There are also playgrounds throughout the zoo, perfect for letting the kids burn off some energy.

12:00 PM – Lunch at the Zoo Café: After your visit to the zoo, enjoy a casual lunch at the Zoo Café, located inside the zoo complex. It's a relaxed setting where families can enjoy simple, kid-friendly meals like sandwiches and salads while watching the animals.

Afternoon: Interactive Science Fun

1:30 PM – Visit the Natural History Museum: After lunch, head to the Natural History Museum (located in the Old Town). This museum is perfect for families with children who love science and nature. The exhibits feature everything from dinosaurs and fossils to minerals and Slovak wildlife. The interactive displays and touchable exhibits will engage younger visitors, making learning fun for everyone.

3:00 PM – Take a Ride on the Funicular Railway: For a fun family experience, take the funicular railway up to Železná Studienka in the foothills of the Little Carpathians. The ride itself is a thrilling experience for children, and once at the top, you can enjoy beautiful views of the city and the surrounding nature. There are several family-friendly walking trails in the area, perfect for a short hike or picnic.

Evening: Fun Dinner and a Relaxing Evening

5:30 PM – Dinner at Hradná Reštaurácia: After a day full of adventure, treat the family to dinner at Hradná Reštaurácia, located near the castle. This family-friendly restaurant offers traditional Slovak dishes and a cozy atmosphere, perfect for a relaxed evening with the family.

7:30 PM – Evening at the Danube Promenade: Wrap up the day with a relaxing walk along the Danube Promenade. Kids will enjoy the open space to run around, while parents can relax and enjoy the view. There are plenty of ice cream vendors along the promenade, so stop and treat the kids to a sweet treat as you watch the sunset over the river.

Day 3: Adventures on the Water and Interactive Play

Morning: Water Fun and Scenic Views

9:00 AM – Breakfast at Café Ernst: Start the day at Café Ernst, another family-friendly spot known for its delicious coffee, pastries, and fresh juices. Enjoy a relaxed breakfast with a variety of options to satisfy every family member's tastes.

10:00 AM – Boat Ride on the Danube River: Today, take a boat cruise on the Danube River. It's a great way to see Bratislava from a different perspective, and children will love the chance to be out on the water. There are several boat tours available, including family-friendly options that offer commentary about the landmarks along the river, such as the Bratislava Castle and UFO Bridge.

- Tip: Choose a shorter cruise for younger children or one with a stop at Devin Castle if you want to combine nature and history.

Afternoon: Play and Explore

12:00 PM – Lunch at Bratislava Flagship Market: For lunch, head to Bratislava Flagship Market, a food hall offering a variety of food stalls, perfect for picky eaters. You can try everything from burgers and pizzas to traditional Slovak dishes and pastries. It's casual and family-friendly, so it's great for everyone to enjoy what they like.

1:30 PM – Visit the Interactive Children's Museum: After lunch, head to the Interactive Children's Museum, which is designed to keep kids engaged while learning through play. The museum features hands-on exhibits where children can explore different fields like art, science, and history in an interactive way. It's a perfect stop for younger children to enjoy while learning about the world around them.

Evening: Dinner and Relaxation

5:30 PM – Dinner at Slovenská Reštaurácia: For your evening meal, visit Slovenská Reštaurácia, a traditional Slovak restaurant that offers hearty meals in a cozy setting. Try dishes like *sviečková* (beef with creamy sauce) or *pečená kačica* (roast duck), both of which are sure to please both adults and children.

7:00 PM – Relaxing Evening in the City: End the day with a quiet family walk through Bratislava's Old Town, where the buildings are lit up at night. This is a great time for the family to reflect on the day's adventures, or you can enjoy a family-friendly activity like ice cream or a visit to a local park.

Day 4: Nature, Relaxation, and Sweet Treats

Morning: Nature and Relaxation

9:00 AM – Breakfast at the Hotel or Local Café: For your final day in Bratislava, start with a relaxed breakfast either at your hotel or at a nearby café, enjoying a range of options to suit the family's preferences.

10:00 AM – Visit the Botanical Garden: Spend the morning at Botanical Garden, a peaceful escape from the hustle and bustle of the city. The garden is a lovely spot for a leisurely walk, with plenty of room for the kids to explore. There are ponds, flowerbeds, and shaded areas to enjoy, and you can even bring a picnic if you wish.

Afternoon: Sweet Treats and Last-Minute Fun

12:00 PM – Sweet Treats at The Chocolate Museum: Stop by the Chocolate Museum for a sweet treat! This interactive museum offers the history of chocolate, how it's made, and provides kids with the opportunity to sample different types of chocolate. They even offer workshops where children can make their own chocolate.

1:30 PM – Lunch at Café Špitálka: Enjoy a family-friendly lunch at Café Špitálka, where you can sample Slovak-style dishes with a contemporary twist. It's a great spot for kids to try some local flavors in a relaxed environment.

Evening: Last Dinner and Family Photos

4:30 PM – Dinner at Savoy Restaurant: For your final dinner in Bratislava, indulge in a fine dining experience at Savoy Restaurant. This elegant restaurant offers a mix of Slovak and international dishes, making it a great place to end your family trip with a delicious meal.

6:00 PM – Family Photos at the UFO Observation Deck: Take a ride up to the UFO Observation Deck for breathtaking views of the city. It's the perfect place to take some family photos against the stunning backdrop of Bratislava's skyline and the Danube River before heading home.

Romantic Weekend Getaway

Romantic Weekend Getaway in Bratislava

Bratislava, with its charming streets, picturesque landscapes, and rich history, is an ideal destination for a romantic weekend getaway. Whether you're looking to explore the city's historic landmarks, enjoy intimate moments in peaceful parks, or indulge in exquisite dining, this city offers everything you need to create unforgettable memories. This itinerary will guide you through a perfect romantic weekend filled with activities that will leave you and your partner relaxed, connected, and in love with the beauty of Bratislava.

Day 1: Exploring the Old Town and Scenic Views

Morning: A Cozy Breakfast and Stroll Through the Old Town

9:00 AM – Breakfast at Café Mayer: Start your romantic weekend with a leisurely breakfast at Café Mayer, one of the oldest coffee houses in Bratislava. The warm, elegant setting offers a perfect atmosphere for couples to enjoy a cozy breakfast together. Treat yourselves to freshly brewed coffee, delicious pastries, and Slovak specialties, such as *trdelník* (sweet pastry) and *koláče* (traditional Slovak cakes).

10:00 AM – Bratislava Castle and Gardens: After breakfast, take a short walk up to Bratislava Castle, which offers breathtaking views of the city, the Danube River, and the surrounding hills. Stroll through the castle's beautiful gardens, where you can enjoy some quiet moments together, surrounded by flowers and greenery. The castle itself is a beautiful place to explore with its historical exhibits and impressive courtyards. Don't forget to take in the panoramic view of the city from the castle's terrace.

11:30 AM – Walk to St. Martin's Cathedral: Take a romantic walk down to St. Martin's Cathedral, one of the most important historical sites in the city. As you stroll through the cobbled streets of the Old Town, enjoy the beautiful architecture and peaceful ambiance. The cathedral, with its impressive Gothic design, provides a tranquil setting to admire the beauty of Bratislava's medieval past. Inside, you'll find a serene atmosphere perfect for quiet reflection.

Afternoon: Explore Old Town and Relax Together

1:00 PM – Lunch at Modrá Hviezda: For lunch, head to Modrá Hviezda, a charming restaurant nestled in the Old Town. The intimate atmosphere and traditional Slovak cuisine make it a wonderful spot for a romantic meal. Indulge in local dishes like *bryndzové halušky* (potato dumplings with sheep cheese) or a lighter option such as *kapustnica* (sauerkraut soup). The restaurant's cozy vibe makes it a perfect place to relax and savor a meal with your partner.

2:30 PM – Romantic Walk Along the Danube River: After lunch, take a leisurely walk along the Danube Promenade. The peaceful riverside setting is ideal for couples, with scenic views of the river and the surrounding landscape. You can sit by the river, enjoy the quiet, and even have a chat while watching the boats sail by. There are several cafés and benches along the way where you can take a break and enjoy each other's company in a tranquil setting.

4:00 PM – Visit the Blue Church (St. Elizabeth's Church): A short walk from the Old Town will bring you to the Blue Church, also known as St. Elizabeth's Church. Its striking blue color and unique Art Nouveau architecture make it one of Bratislava's most beloved landmarks. It's a beautiful spot for a peaceful moment together, and the intricate design inside is something to admire. It's a hidden gem in the city that often surprises visitors with its charm.

Evening: A Romantic Dinner with a View

6:30 PM – Dinner at UFO Restaurant: For a truly memorable evening, book a table at the UFO Restaurant, located atop the UFO Tower. This unique dining experience offers spectacular views of Bratislava and the Danube River from the observation deck. The romantic atmosphere and stunning panorama make it the perfect spot for a special dinner. The menu offers a variety of international and Slovak dishes, and the fine dining experience ensures a night to remember.

8:00 PM – Sunset Views from UFO Observation Deck: After dinner, head to the UFO Observation Deck for an unforgettable sunset. The panoramic view from the top of the tower is simply breathtaking, providing the perfect backdrop for a romantic moment. As the sun sets over the city, enjoy the quiet beauty of the Danube and the sparkling lights of Bratislava. It's a stunning way to end the day.

9:00 PM – Nightcap at a Cozy Wine Bar: To continue the romantic evening, visit Vinotéka u Sudu, a cozy wine bar located in the Old Town. Enjoy a glass of local Slovak wine in a relaxed and intimate setting. The warm atmosphere of the wine bar is perfect for unwinding after a day of sightseeing, and it provides a lovely spot to reflect on your experiences together.

Day 2: Adventure, Culture, and Relaxation

Morning: Visit to Devin Castle and Nature Walk

9:00 AM – Breakfast at Urban House: On your second day, start with a relaxed breakfast at Urban House, known for its cozy atmosphere and delicious breakfast options. Choose from a variety of fresh pastries, eggs, smoothie bowls, and strong coffee to get ready for an exciting day of exploration.

10:00 AM – Visit to Devin Castle: Take a short bus or taxi ride to Devin Castle, located just outside the city. Perched on a cliff at the confluence of the Danube and Morava rivers, the castle offers spectacular views of the surrounding nature. Take a romantic stroll through the ruins, explore the castle's history, and enjoy the quiet, scenic landscape. The castle is surrounded by forests and walking trails, making it a perfect place for a peaceful nature walk together.

12:00 PM – Picnic in the Devín Region: After exploring the castle, take some time to enjoy a picnic near the river or in the nearby park. You can bring your own food or pick up something from a local market. The peaceful environment, combined with the natural beauty of the area, creates an idyllic setting for a romantic moment.

Afternoon: Cultural Experience and Relaxation

2:00 PM – Return to the City for the Slovak National Gallery: Head back to the city and visit the Slovak National Gallery, a wonderful place to enjoy art together. The gallery showcases Slovak and international art, from classical works to contemporary exhibitions. Take your time exploring the galleries and discussing the art, and enjoy the peaceful atmosphere inside.

3:30 PM – Tea or Coffee at the Café in the Gallery: After touring the gallery, relax with a cup of tea or coffee at the gallery's café. The cozy, modern space is the perfect place to unwind while enjoying a quiet moment with your partner.

Evening: Romantic Dinner and Moonlit Walk

6:30 PM – Dinner at Savoy Restaurant: For a fine dining experience, enjoy dinner at Savoy Restaurant, located inside the Hotel Carlton. The elegant, historic atmosphere makes it a perfect place for a romantic evening. Indulge in beautifully crafted dishes, with an emphasis on local ingredients and Slovak cuisine, paired with a selection of wines from the region.

8:00 PM – Moonlit Walk in the Old Town: After dinner, take a romantic moonlit stroll through the Old Town. The streets are beautifully lit at night, and the architecture looks even more magical under the soft glow of the streetlights. Walk hand-in-hand through the narrow alleys, past charming squares, and enjoy the peace and beauty of the city at night.

9:00 PM – Drinks at a Cocktail Bar: End your romantic getaway with a nightcap at one of Bratislava's stylish cocktail bars. Head to The KGB Bar, a quirky, cozy place offering creative cocktails in a fun setting, or visit KC Dunaj, a popular bar with a laid-back atmosphere where you can enjoy a drink while reflecting on your weekend adventures.

Chapter 14. Resources

Useful Websites and Apps

Useful Websites and Apps for a Trip to Bratislava

Planning your trip to Bratislava can be even easier with the help of various websites and apps that provide helpful information, guide you through the city, and make navigating local transportation and attractions a breeze. Below is a curated list of useful resources for visitors:

---

1. Official Tourism Websites

- Bratislava Tourist Board
  Website: www.visitbratislava.com
  The official site for tourists visiting Bratislava. It offers detailed information on attractions, events, recommended tours, accommodation, and other useful details like transport options and local festivals.

- Slovakia Tourism
  Website: www.slovakia.travel
  This website provides a comprehensive guide to all that Slovakia offers, including regional highlights, cultural events, and outdoor activities, perfect for planning day trips from Bratislava.

---

2. Transportation & Navigation Apps

- Google Maps
  App: Available on Android and iOS
  Google Maps is essential for navigating Bratislava's streets and public transportation. You can use it to find walking routes, public transport options, and nearby attractions.

- IDOS
  App: Available on Android and iOS
  This app provides public transport timetables for Bratislava and across Slovakia, including buses, trams, and trains, helping you plan your journeys effectively.

- Bolt
  App: Available on Android and iOS
  Bolt is a popular ride-hailing service in Bratislava, ideal for getting around the city quickly and conveniently.

- Uber
  App: Available on Android and iOS

Uber is also available in Bratislava, providing an alternative to traditional taxis for getting around the city.

---

3. Cultural & Attraction Apps

- Bratislava Card
  Website: www.bratislava-card.com
  This app is designed for tourists and gives you access to discounted entry to many attractions in Bratislava, including museums, galleries, and cultural sites, as well as free public transport.

- TripAdvisor
  App: Available on Android and iOS
  TripAdvisor is a go-to app for researching and reading reviews about Bratislava's restaurants, attractions, and activities, making it easy to plan your day.

- Viator
  App: Available on Android and iOS
  Viator helps you discover and book guided tours, activities, and experiences in and around Bratislava, including boat cruises on the Danube River and wine-tasting tours in the Small Carpathian Wine Region.

---

4. Restaurant & Food Apps

- Zomato
  App: Available on Android and iOS
  Zomato helps you find restaurants, cafes, and bars in Bratislava. You can browse menus, check reviews, and make reservations directly through the app.

- TheFork
  App: Available on Android and iOS
  TheFork is another great app to help you discover dining options in Bratislava, and it often includes options for making restaurant reservations online.

---

5. Event & Activity Apps

- Eventbrite
  App: Available on Android and iOS
  Eventbrite is perfect for finding events happening around Bratislava during your visit, whether you're interested in concerts, theater performances, or local festivals.

- Meetup
  App: Available on Android and iOS
  Meetup is ideal for discovering social events, group activities, and interest-based gatherings. It's great for travelers who want to connect with locals or fellow tourists.

---

6. Currency and Budgeting Apps

- Revolut
  App: Available on Android and iOS
  Revolut is a great app for managing money abroad, offering low-fee currency exchange, budgeting tools, and the ability to spend in multiple currencies without additional charges.

- XE Currency
  App: Available on Android and iOS
  XE Currency helps you track live exchange rates for the Slovak Koruna (Slovakia's currency) and provides an easy-to-use converter, so you can budget while traveling.

---

7. Weather Apps

- AccuWeather
  App: Available on Android and iOS
  AccuWeather gives accurate, real-time weather forecasts for Bratislava, so you can plan your outdoor activities accordingly.

- The Weather Channel
  App: Available on Android and iOS
  The Weather Channel provides detailed weather updates and alerts for Bratislava, helping you stay prepared for any weather conditions during your trip.

---

8. Language Apps

- Google Translate
  App: Available on Android and iOS
  Google Translate is incredibly helpful if you don't speak Slovak. The app allows you to translate text and speech in real-time, and it also offers offline translation features.

- Duolingo
  App: Available on Android and iOS
  Duolingo is a fun and interactive app to learn some basic Slovak phrases before you visit, helping you feel more confident in communicating with locals.

9. Parking & Transport Apps

- Parkopedia
  App: Available on Android and iOS
  Parkopedia helps you find parking in Bratislava, whether you're looking for public parking lots or private parking garages, with real-time availability updates.

- Sygic Travel
  App: Available on Android and iOS
  Sygic Travel offers city guides, GPS navigation, and offline maps, making it a great app for planning trips to attractions and getting around Bratislava.

Contact Information for Tourist Offices and Services

Contact Information for Tourist Offices and Services in Bratislava

When visiting Bratislava, it's always useful to have access to local tourist offices and services. Below is a list of the main tourist offices and important contact information to help you plan your trip, find information, and make inquiries during your stay.

1. Bratislava Tourist Board (Visit Bratislava)

The official tourism board provides comprehensive information on everything related to tourism in the city, from attractions to tours, transport, and cultural events.

- Website: www.visitbratislava.com
- Phone: +421 2 5935 7800
- Email: info@visitbratislava.com
- Address: Klobučnícka 2, 811 01 Bratislava, Slovakia
- Opening Hours:
- Monday to Friday: 9:00 AM – 6:00 PM
- Saturday: 9:00 AM – 3:00 PM
- Sunday: Closed

2. Bratislava Information Center (Tourist Information Center)

The main information center located in the heart of the Old Town provides brochures, maps, and assistance to tourists.

- Website: www.visitbratislava.com
- Phone: +421 2 5935 7800
- Email: info@visitbratislava.com
- Address: Primaciálne námestie 3, 814 99 Bratislava, Slovakia
- Opening Hours:
- Monday to Friday: 9:00 AM – 6:00 PM

- Saturday: 9:00 AM – 3:00 PM
- Sunday: Closed

3. Bratislava Airport (M. R. Štefánik International Airport)

For travelers arriving at or departing from Bratislava Airport, the airport's customer service is available to assist with flight information, transport options, and any other inquiries.

- Website: www.bts.aero
- Phone: +421 2 3301 7300
- Email: info@bts.aero
- Address: Letisko M. R. Štefánika, 823 11 Bratislava, Slovakia

4. Train Station (Bratislava Hlavná Stanica) Tourist Information Desk

For assistance with train tickets, local transportation, and regional travel, the tourist information desk at the main train station is a helpful resource.

- Phone: +421 2 3261 3211
- Email: info@zssk.sk (for Slovak Railways inquiries)
- Address: Námestie Franza Kafku 2, 811 04 Bratislava, Slovakia
- Opening Hours:
- Monday to Friday: 8:00 AM – 5:00 PM
- Saturday: 8:00 AM – 12:00 PM
- Sunday: Closed

5. Slovak National Tourism Center (SLOVENSKÁ CESTOVNÁ AGENTÚRA)

This national tourism service helps travelers with information about Slovakia's regions, tourist attractions, and activities.

- Website: www.sacr.sk
- Phone: +421 2 5934 2755
- Email: sacr@sacr.sk
- Address: Karadžičova 2, 821 08 Bratislava, Slovakia

6. Bratislava Card – Tourist Pass

For discounts on public transport, entrance to museums, and other attractions in the city, the Bratislava Card is available at various locations in the city and online.

- Website: www.bratislava-card.com
- Phone: +421 2 5935 7800
- Email: info@visitbratislava.com
- Address: Klobučnícka 2, 811 01 Bratislava, Slovakia

7. Tourist Information at the Bratislava Bus Station

If you're arriving or departing by bus, the tourist information desk at the Bratislava Bus Station can help with local transit information, sightseeing, and tickets.

- Phone: +421 2 6353 2161
- Address: Autobusová stanica Mlynské nivy, Mlynské nivy 31, 821 09 Bratislava, Slovakia
- Opening Hours:
- Monday to Friday: 7:00 AM – 7:00 PM
- Saturday: 8:00 AM – 4:00 PM
- Sunday: Closed

8. Bratislava Public Transport Authority (DPB)

For public transport information, including schedules, routes, and tickets for buses, trams, and trolleybuses in Bratislava, contact the local public transport authority.

- Website: www.dpb.sk
- Phone: +421 2 2047 2222
- Email: info@dpb.sk
- Address: Karadžičova 8, 813 61 Bratislava, Slovakia

9. Taxi Services in Bratislava

For reliable and licensed taxi services, you can contact any of the following providersTaxi Bratislava

- Phone: +421 2 4445 5555
- Website: www.taxibratislava.sk
- AAA Taxi
- Phone: +421 2 3300 3300
- Website: www.aaataxi.sk
- Taxi Karpatia
- Phone: +421 911 400 400
- Website: www.taxikarpatiask.sk

10. Local Tour Operators

For guided tours and day trips in and around Bratislava, these tour operators provide expert guidance and personalized experiencesBratislava City Tours

- Website: www.bratislava-city-tours.sk
- Phone: +421 948 199 719
- Slovak Private Tours
- Website: www.slovakprivatetours.com
- Phone: +421 903 903 254
- Travel Fan
- Website: www.travelfan.sk
- Phone: +421 2 6381 4432

11. Emergency Numbers

It's essential to have the emergency contact information on hand while traveling.

- Police: 112 (EU-wide emergency number) or 155 (Slovak police)
- Ambulance: 155
- Fire Department: 150
- Emergency Help for Foreigners (Slovak Ministry of Foreign Affairs): +421 2 5978 3032

Bonus

Language Tips: Basic Slovak Phrases for Travelers

Language Tips: Basic Slovak Phrases for Travelers

While many people in Bratislava speak English, especially in tourist areas, learning a few basic Slovak phrases can make your trip more enjoyable and help you connect with locals. Slovaks are known for appreciating efforts made by visitors to speak their language, and knowing just a few simple words and phrases can go a long way. Here are some useful Slovak phrases to help you during your visit:

Basic Greetings and Polite Expressions

- Ahoj! (Ah-hoy) – *Hello!* Use this informal greeting when meeting friends or people you know.
- Dobrý deň! (Doh-bree dyen) – *Good day!* A more formal greeting, suitable for addressing strangers or in professional settings.
- Dobrý večer! (Doh-bree veh-cher) – *Good evening!*
- Zbohom! (Zboh-hom) – *Goodbye!* A formal way to say goodbye.
- Čau! (Chow) – *Bye!* A casual way of saying goodbye among friends.
- Ako sa máš? (Ah-ko sah mahsh?) – *How are you?* A casual greeting you can use with friends. The more formal version would be "Ako sa máte?" (Ah-ko sah mah-teh?).
- Ďakujem (Dya-koo-yem) – *Thank you.* Use this to show appreciation for services or help.
- Ďakujem veľmi pekne (Dya-koo-yem vel-mee pek-nye) – *Thank you very much.*
- Prosím (Pro-seem) – *Please* A polite word used when making requests.
- Prepáčte (Preh-paht-ye) – *Excuse me / I'm sorry* Use this to apologize or to get someone's attention.

Basic Phrases for Getting Around

- Kde je...? (Kde yeh) – *Where is...?* Use this to ask for directions, for example, "Kde je autobusová stanica?" (Where is the bus station?).
- Koľko to stojí? (Kol-ko toh stoy-yee?) – *How much does this cost?*
- Môžem zaplatiť? (Mwah-zh-em zap-lah-teet?) – *Can I pay?*
- Kde je toaleta? (Kde yeh toh-ah-leh-tah?) – *Where is the toilet?*

- Hovoríte po anglicky? (Ho-voh-ree-teh poh ahn-glit-skee?) – *Do you speak English?*
- Neviem po slovensky. (Neh-vyehm poh sloh-ven-skee.) – *I don't speak Slovak.* A helpful phrase if you're struggling to understand.

Dining and Ordering Food

- Mám hlad. (Mahm hlad) – *I'm hungry.* Useful if you're looking for somewhere to eat.
- Môžem si objednať? (Mwah-zh-em see oh-byed-nat?) – *Can I order?*
- Máte jedálny lístok? (Mah-teh yeh-dahl-nee leesk-tok?) – *Do you have a menu?*
- Čo mi odporúčate? (Choh mee od-po-roo-cha-te?) – *What do you recommend?*
- Voda (Voh-dah) – *Water* If you prefer still water, you can ask for "voda bez bubliniek" (still water), or if you want sparkling water, you can say "voda s bublinkami" (sparkling water).
- Pivo (Pee-voh) – *Beer* Slovakia is known for its beer culture, and ordering a local beer is a great experience.

Useful Phrases for Shopping

- Koľko to stojí? (Kol-ko toh stoy-yee?) – *How much is this?*
- Máte zľavy? (Mah-teh zlyah-vee?) – *Do you have discounts?*
- Kde je najbližší obchod? (Kde yeh nay-blee-zhee ohb-chod?) – *Where is the nearest shop?*
- Chcel(a) by som… (Htsell(a) bee soh-m) – *I would like…*
  Use this when requesting something. For example, "Chcel by som tričko." (I would like a T-shirt.)

Emergency Phrases

- Pomoc! (Poh-mots) – *Help!* A vital phrase to know in case you need urgent assistance.
- Volajte políciu! (Voh-lah-yeh poh-lee-tsy-oo) – *Call the police!*
- Stratil(a) som peňaženku. (Strah-til/ah sohm pen-yah-zen-koo) – *I lost my wallet.*
- Som stratený/stratená. (Som strah-teh-nee/strah-teh-nah) – *I am lost.*
  "Stratený" is for men, and "stratená" is for women.

Numbers (1-10)

- 1 – Jeden (Yeh-den)
- 2 – Dva (Dvah)
- 3 – Tri (Tree)
- 4 – Štyri (Shtee-ree)

- 5 – Päť (Pyaht)
- 6 – Šesť (Shesht)
- 7 – Sedem (Seh-dem)
- 8 – Osem (Oh-sem)
- 9 – Deväť (Deh-vyeht)
- 10 – Desať (Deh-saht)

Knowing numbers will come in handy when you are shopping, paying for services, or using public transportation.

Pronunciation Tips

- Vowels: Slovak vowels are pronounced clearly.
    - A is pronounced like "ah" (as in "father").
    - E is pronounced like "eh" (as in "bed").
    - I is pronounced like "ee" (as in "see").
    - O is pronounced like "oh" (as in "go").
    - U is pronounced like "oo" (as in "moon").
- Consonants: Slovak has some consonants that may seem unfamiliar, such as č (ch in "chocolate"), š (sh in "ship"), ž (zh in "treasure"), and ň (ny in "canyon").
- Accents: In written Slovak, accents are important because they change the meaning of words. For instance, "slovo" means "word," but "slová" means "words."

Travel Journal

Date	Destination/Stop	Key Activities/Excursions	Memorable Moments	Food Tried/Restaurants	Thoughts & Reflections	Photos Taken (Yes/No)
Day 1						
Day 2						

Day 3						
Day 4						
Day 5						
Day 6						
Day 7						
Packing List:		Special Memories to Remember:			Important Contacts/Information	

Dear reader,

First and foremost, thank you for choosing this guide to help you explore the beautiful city of Bratislava. Writing this book has been a journey close to my heart, one filled with countless hours of research, travel, and personal exploration of the city's hidden gems. As someone who deeply cares about sharing authentic experiences, every word written here has been carefully crafted to offer you the best possible insights to ensure your visit is nothing short of extraordinary.

However, the true success of this guide lies in your experience. If you've found the information valuable, if you feel inspired to explore Bratislava's cobbled streets and picturesque landmarks, I would be so grateful for your positive review. Your feedback means more than just a few kind words — it is the heartbeat of my journey as a travel guide writer.

Your review not only encourages me, but it helps others who are seeking to make the most of their trip to this wonderful city. It tells me that my effort, the time I dedicated to personally experiencing the wonders of Bratislava, and the resources invested — both financially and emotionally — are truly making a difference in someone's travel plans. Your words are my motivation to continue writing, researching, and improving my guides so that future travelers have access to even more enriched, personalized, and useful resources.

Visiting Bratislava, exploring its culture, its sights, and understanding its soul was a personal investment I was eager to make, and I've poured my heart into ensuring that you get the best of it. This book is not just about what's on the surface, but about capturing the essence of the city, the quiet moments, the unforgettable experiences, and the stories of people that make Bratislava the unique gem it is.

If you've enjoyed your time with this book, your review is not just feedback; it is the greatest gift you can give to me as a writer. It's a chance for you to let others know how this guide helped you discover the beauty of Bratislava — a city full of wonder, hidden treasures, and unforgettable memories.

Thank you for taking the time to read, explore, and, hopefully, share your thoughts with the world. Your support makes it all worthwhile, and I look forward to hearing about your own adventures and discoveries in Bratislava!

With sincere gratitude and appreciation,

Rachel J. Pugh

Printed in Great Britain
by Amazon